SCHOOL COUNSELLORS WORKING
WITH YOUNG PEOPLE AND STAFF

by the same author

Feeling Like Crap
Young People and the Meaning of Self-Esteem
ISBN 978 1 84310 682 1
eISBN 978 1 84642 819 7

Working with Anger and Young People
ISBN 978 1 84310 466 7
eISBN 978 1 84642 538 7

Listening to Young People in School,
Youth Work and Counselling
ISBN 978 1 85302 909 7
eISBN 978 1 84642 201 0

Young People, Death and the Unfairness of Everything
ISBN 978 1 84905 320 4
eISBN 978 0 85700 662 2

Young People and the Curse of Ordinariness
ISBN 978 1 84905 185 9
eISBN 978 0 85700 407 9

Young People in Love and in Hate
ISBN 978 1 84905 055 5
eISBN 978 0 85700 202 0

SCHOOL COUNSELLORS WORKING WITH YOUNG PEOPLE AND STAFF

A WHOLE-SCHOOL APPROACH

Nick Luxmoore

Jessica Kingsley *Publishers*
London and Philadelphia

A version of Chapter 10 was published in the June 2012
BACP Children and Young People journal.

First published in 2014
by Jessica Kingsley Publishers
73 Collier Street
London N1 9BE, UK
and
400 Market Street, Suite 400
Philadelphia, PA 19106, USA

www.jkp.com

Library of Congress Cataloging in Publication Data
A CIP catalog record for this book is available from the Library of Congress

British Library Cataloguing in Publication Data
A CIP catalogue record for this book is available from the British Library

ISBN 978 1 84905 460 7
eISBN 978 0 85700 838 1

Printed and bound in Great Britain

For
Jane Campbell

CONTENTS

ACKNOWLEDGEMENTS

A version of Chapter 10 was originally published in the June 2012 *BACP Children and Young People* journal.

This book is the product of work developed with the support of many people, especially the headteachers I've worked with and particularly the ones by whom I've been managed – Bill Berry, Bernard Clarke, Mary Fitzpatrick, Nick Young and Simon Spiers. The work has also been possible because of the supervisors who've supported and taught me – Sue Douglas and Jane Campbell. I'm grateful to colleagues at King Alfred's Academy, Wantage, for supporting my current work, especially to Adam Arnell, Kate Baker and Diane Jones who organise the training. I'm also grateful to Kathy Peto, Debbie Lee, Professor Chris Mowles and Jane Campbell for reading and commenting on drafts of this book. Especial thanks (always) to Kathy, Frances and Julia.

1 INTRODUCTION

'So you're the counsellor then? I don't think we've had one of them before. Or if we have, I've never seen them! Anyway, pleased to meet you. I can think of a few of our youngsters who'll be coming your way. In fact, there are probably a few members of staff who could do with your services as well. No, only joking! I don't suppose you're allowed to do counselling for staff, are you?'

—

This book describes why and how the processes and understandings of counselling will be at the heart of any good school. Working with others, counsellors can help to develop cultures in which young people and staff feel more confident and valued than they would otherwise feel and, of course, when people feel confident and valued, they not only lead happier lives but also tend to do better academically.

There are a few training courses for counsellors wanting to work with young people, but I know of only one training course specifically for counsellors wanting to work with schools. Instead, school counsellors have to learn on the job, adapting whatever they've learned from other contexts. I've worked for more than 26 years as a school counsellor with young people aged 11–18 and with staff aged 22–65. It's been a privilege but, as this book describes, there have been important lessons to learn. So I'm always delighted when I hear that a school has decided to appoint a counsellor, but then I get nervous, worrying about how the counsellor will interpret the brief. Will he or she work with the whole institution as well as with individuals, making counselling and the understandings of counselling available to everyone? Or will this particular counsellor choose to remain mysterious and peripheral, narrowly involved in the life of the school, afraid of breaking some imaginary rule whereby counsellors must keep themselves apart? Will counselling in this school come to be seen as shameful and secretive, available only to the weird and the weak? Or will people start to feel that the service is for everyone because counselling is fast becoming a normal part of school life, with everybody starting to think that they might become quite good counsellors themselves? There are wonderfully creative opportunities for counsellors to make a difference in schools. But there are dangers.

Different schools expect different things from the person they call the counsellor. In some parts of the world, the 'counsellor' is the person offering 'guidance'. In others, the 'counsellor' helps out with a tutorial programme or with outdoor activities, helps young people with learning difficulties or provides careers advice. This is all good work but you don't need to be trained as a counsellor to do these things: teachers can do them perfectly well. Instead, this book is about school counsellors as *therapists*, taking account of a person's external circumstances but aiming, ultimately, to work with a person's internal world, a world of unconscious defences holding anxieties at bay. It's a book about what goes on in the privacy of the counselling room; about what helps and hinders the therapeutic process.

But it's also about what goes on *outside* that room because, as Chapters 2, 3, 4 and 5 describe, school counselling relationships are inseparable from their context: the individual and the group are interdependent. Foulkes (1948) writes that 'Each individual – itself an artificial, though plausible, abstraction – is basically and centrally determined, inevitably, by the world in which he lives, by the community, the group, of which he forms a part' (p.10). So whenever young people are complaining of bullying, for example, that bullying will usually be an expression of group as well as individual anxieties: anxieties about difference, intelligence, strength, attractiveness. Whenever sexual teasing between individuals is rife, there's likely to be a general anxiety in the corridors and staffroom about sex and sexuality. And there'll be plenty of other anxieties in the institutional mix as well – anxieties about status, aloneness, visibility, power, failure, success – with some individuals having what Bion (1961) calls a 'valency', an aptitude for unwittingly picking up and expressing these anxieties on behalf of others as well as themselves. 'The individual identity of each one of us', writes Pines (1998), 'is constituted by intrapsychic, interpersonal and transpersonal processes; the boundaries of the individual extend far beyond those of the corporeal self' (p.25).

In this sense, young people and staff come to counselling on behalf of the school as well as themselves. They come with a sense of what's fair and unfair, of belonging and not belonging, of feeling looked after and not looked after. They bring the issues preoccupying the school: a disparate collection of individuals all worried about fairness, belonging and being looked after. Young people's anxieties will reflect and express the anxieties of staff. For example, there's likely to be a lot of anger enacted by students if the staffroom is full of unexpressed anger. There's likely to be a lot of self-harming amongst students if teachers are scared and unsure how to respond to self-harming. And through the wonders of projective identification, members of staff will, in turn, tend to pick up and express the anxieties of students, feeling angry and unloved, burdened with other people's expectations and, at the end of another long day, worried about the future themselves.

Hinshelwood (2001) writes that because the prevailing culture of the institution affects the individual, 'that culture should itself be a part of the therapeutic investigation' (p.54). I agree. A school counsellor needs to be paying attention to and trying to affect whatever's happening at an institutional as well as individual level, not least because a young person's experience of living for seven hours a day in an institution that supports or ignores, values or scorns him will be as powerfully therapeutic or anti-therapeutic as any work going on behind the closed doors of a counselling room. Lanyado (2004) writes that 'the therapeutic environment in which the therapy sessions themselves take place is as important in facilitating change as the other tools in the therapist's clinical bag' (p.57). Winnicott (1975) goes further, describing how, for some young people, the environment or 'placement' in which they find themselves is *more* important than their work with a therapist.

Because of this, a counsellor needs to be out and about, saying hello to people, taking the institutional temperature and having an effect on it. As a school counsellor, my own repertoire of involvements beyond the counselling room has included organising sex education (Luxmoore 2010), running groups (Luxmoore 2000, 2002, 2008), developing student consultation, supervising and training staff, managing peer support schemes (Luxmoore 2000, 2002), recruiting and supervising volunteer counsellors and running workshops for parents. Whatever their effectiveness, these involvements have been intended to have a positive effect on the school culture, assuaging anxieties and thereby lessening the damaging impact of those anxieties on individuals.

Young people dread being shamed, so when their trust has been abused at home or at school, they're understandably wary of trusting anyone associated with home or with school. They might be prepared to talk with a counsellor, but if the prevailing school culture decrees that counselling is for 'weirdos', 'psychos' or 'people with problems', then doing so will require courage and secrecy because of the threat of other people finding out. Young people might put some trust in a counsellor but only on condition that he or she has nothing to do with their parents, teachers or peers. Perhaps with situations like these in mind, McGinnis and Jenkins (2011) write that 'A counsellor can be very effective working with the pastoral support structure of a school but it is often the "independent" nature of the service that gives pupils confidence in having counselling with someone who does not play a part in the rest of their school life' (p.16).

This is problematic. In schools where there's little or no personal safety and feelings are seen as weaknesses to be mocked, keeping the counselling service 'independent' may be a necessary short-term measure to protect young people whose trust has been abused. But in the long-term, the service has to become integrated into the school as a whole in order to change the culture. Like any other school department, the counselling service will always need a *degree* of independence but, in the long run, it'll be doing nobody any favours if it sets out to be independent, determinedly apart from mainstream school life. Where people are mocked for using the counselling service, the counsellor has to set about changing the way people think about counselling by demystifying the service (see Chapter 3), putting it at the *heart* of school life rather than allowing it to remain marginalised, the object of everyone's hostile projections.

Perhaps in the belief that being 'independent' is the name of the game, there are some school counsellors who remain deliberately aloof, the door firmly shut, believing that confidentiality will inevitably be compromised if they're seen talking with teachers in the corridor or joining in with normal school activities. The implication of this is that confidentiality is such a brittle thing that a counsellor would only have to meet a teacher in the corridor to find herself telling all! There's also the implication that teachers are untrustworthy and incapable of supporting distressed students themselves when, in fact, most teachers do this on a daily basis and with far more students than a counsellor will ever meet.

Confidentiality matters, but remaining aloof and refusing to engage with these issues doesn't help. If some teachers are less respectful of confidentiality than they should be, then they'll only get better at managing confidentiality by coming into contact with a counsellor who maintains a normally interactive relationship with them in the corridor while keeping confidential all the things that need to be kept confidential. Perpetuating a split in young people's minds between 'those who can be trusted' and 'those who can't be trusted' is unhelpful. The fact is that we tell different people different things. As Chapter 5 describes, it's perfectly possible for confidentiality to be maintained and for a counsellor to be talking (and *seen* to be talking) with all sorts of other professionals.

This book is also a way of talking with other professionals and confidentiality is therefore an issue. For fear of jeopardising my clients' confidentiality, I could decide to include no case material in the book and stick to dry theorising, but then the danger would be of readers getting no sense of what the work actually feels like. So there has to be a way forward. Faced with the problem, Marzillier (2010) writes: 'I made a decision to…create a disguise, a fiction from the raw material of fact. In this way, the people [in my book] are all real but the account I give of them and of their therapy has been fictionalized' (p.xvi). I like this; so, in the same way, all the people, conversations and dilemmas in this book are true and untrue. The details are all changed – no one would recognise themselves – and in that sense, they're untrue, but the spirit of each person and each situation is completely true.

Along with concerns about confidentiality, it's also argued sometimes that leaving the safety of the counselling room and being seen around school – no longer a blank screen – skews a client's transference to the counsellor; that knowing her outside the counselling room stops young people projecting unconscious material onto the counsellor. Clearly, working with young people in a school isn't the same as working with fee-paying adults in thrice-weekly Kleinian psychoanalysis. However psychoanalytically trained a counsellor may be, the rules of that training have to be adapted considerably to work in a school. School counselling isn't private practice. The counsellor doesn't *happen* to be working in a school, seeing a few people in secret and then going away again. Being a *school* counsellor is about working on many different levels at the same time. Young people have to learn about different kinds of privacy (Luxmoore 2000), about having one kind of conversation in the counselling room, another in the canteen, another in the classroom. They have to learn that adults are multi-faceted: listening intently in the counselling room, eating food and chatting in the canteen, insisting on rules in the classroom. And they have to learn that this is *normal*: no one's pretending or playing a game; people are never just one thing.

So this book is about the counsellor as a visible presence in a school, known by everybody and contributing to the life of a school in many different ways. Of course, that contribution will be constrained by whether the counsellor is full- or (sometimes very) part-time. But the principle remains the same. The mysterious presences hiding themselves away on the sidelines in the name of 'confidentiality' and 'independence' risk losing their jobs if nobody knows what it is that they do or, even, who they are. When budgets have to be cut, it's much easier to cut the job you know nothing about, the person you've never met. Peripatetic counsellors are also likely to be at a disadvantage, coming into school from an agency once a week, forever seen as outsiders, rarely able to affect the quality of relationships in the school because they don't belong to the staffroom and are distanced – most importantly – from the headteacher.

Getting a counselling service started in a school is hard work. I've met counsellors who complain indignantly that their school doesn't take counselling seriously, that they're marginalised or ignored, that the room they've been given is a cupboard under the stairs with paper-thin walls and no heating. I know that this happens and that it makes life difficult but, at the same time, why *should* a school respect and value someone just because they call themselves a counsellor? Or because they happen to have a qualification? Or because they say that they're good at listening? The only way to get respect in a school is by being relentlessly reliable over a long period of time, by appreciating and never undermining staff, by intervening to stop the fight in the corridor, by helping out when the reception area floods and piles of documents have to be rescued, by re-decorating the cupboard under the stairs, making it colourful and cosy and, above all, by doing really excellent work inside it.

I've interviewed many kind, warm-hearted counsellors wanting to work in schools. Without exception, they pride themselves on their ability to listen and empathise, which is fine, except that *everybody* in the school – receptionists, caretakers and canteen staff, to say nothing of teachers and teaching assistants – will also be priding themselves on these abilities. In fact, they'll be taking these abilities for granted.

'What do you see as the difference between listening and counselling?' we ask at interview.

'Well, a counsellor is trained,' says the counsellor, 'trained to listen.'

'But so is everyone at this school!' blurts the headteacher.

'Yes,' says the counsellor, 'but do they listen to people's feelings?'

'Not always,' she replies, 'and that's because of time, because they're busy. They *want* to listen to people's feelings!'

'Feelings about families?'

'Naturally!' she says, irritated. 'My staff are perfectly well aware that people's feelings about their families are important. I want to know, what will you be doing as a counsellor that's different from what the rest of my staff are already doing?'

The question has to be answered. Listening and empathising matter, of course they do. One of the tasks for any counsellor is to bear witness to another person's experience – accepting it, respecting it – and listening is at the heart of this. And without empathising, how else can a counsellor know what's being felt, what's being avoided, what's not being said? But once we've listened and empathised, what then? What else might a counsellor be aiming to do? What turns the conversation into something more deliberately therapeutic?

The middle part of this book describes five key therapeutic aims in work with young people and staff. Achieving any of these might represent a successful therapeutic outcome. Chapter 6 describes people learning to speak about rather than enact their anxieties. Chapter 7 describes them going on to develop a capacity to tolerate ambivalence, no longer using splitting as an automatic defence against difficult feelings. Chapter 8 is about becoming less reliant on a 'false' self to protect a 'true' self. Chapter 9 is about developing a sense of personal worth or 'self-esteem'. Chapter 10 describes people learning to bear the anxieties of not knowing why bad things happen in life.

Counsellors need to be therapeutically incisive in order to justify their existence. Merely following another person's lead, listening and trusting that the conversation will somehow end up being worthwhile isn't enough. Usually, young people don't know where the conversation is going or where it needs to go: they're looking to follow rather than lead. Most conversations will therefore be littered with red herrings, avoidances and dead ends as the young person, like any normally defended person, works hard to skirt around or avoid the issues that matter.

Most schools don't really know what to expect when they appoint a counsellor. They may have heard good things from other schools and may want a bit of that for themselves. Or they may have the vague notion that a counsellor will be good at supporting the most disruptive students. They'd quite like a wizard with a magic wand but, beyond that, have little idea of the role's potential. They're happy to be guided by the counsellor once he or she is established and has earned some credibility in the staffroom and corridors *as a therapist.*

It takes time to find ways of contributing to the life of the school beyond the confines of the counselling room. Chapters 11, 12, 13 and 14 describe ways of developing a school counselling service. There are other ways. In fact, the creative possibilities are endless but only emerge once that credibility as a therapist has been earned. I've heard newly appointed counsellors complaining about mistrustful, envious schools wanting proof that their counsellor is making a tangible difference. Evidently, the counsellor has been told to jump through a series of paperwork hoops devised by the school in the hope that this will prove something. This is frustrating, but in schools where the counselling is excellent, it's less likely to happen. These schools already know that the work of the counsellor is excellent because students are saying so and staff are taking notice of this. From her very first day, staff will have been asking students, 'How's it going? How are you getting on with the new counsellor?' They're intrigued. They're not asking for confidential details but they do want to know whether or not to invest further in the counsellor. When they hear good things, they become less suspicious, they relax, only too happy to let the counsellor get on with it. And *that's* when the doors of opportunity start opening: a chance to speak to some governors, an invitation to run some Listening Skills training, a request to help the deputy headteacher think through a tricky situation... And, as if by magic, a much better room has now become available. What's more, there's a rumour that extra money might be available for counselling next year.

Before I was a school counsellor, I was a teacher. It's always been a great help to know the difference between working as a teacher with thirty conscripts, hour after hour, day after day, and working as a counsellor with one consenting volunteer at a time. It helps to know how tiring teaching is, how little thanks teachers get, how resentful of outsiders they become and how few opportunities they get to reflect on their work and its effect on their lives. The school counselling services I've run have therefore been as much for the use of staff as students.

There are two reasons for this. The most obvious reason is simply that members of staff need the counselling service. Just because you happen to be 22 or 42 or 62 years old, you don't stop feeling things or finding certain relationships difficult; life doesn't necessarily get any easier or clearer; the past is still important and the future still unknown. A distressed member of staff is as disruptive as a distressed student and any member of staff missing work because of so-called 'stress' costs the school a lot of money. Offering the counselling service to staff as well as to students makes economic as well as practical sense, therefore.

The second reason is that when the counselling service exists only for students, it's easy for members of staff to portray it as something for the young or for those not coping with life in some way. Privately jealous, they defend against their own need for support by asserting that, at their age, they wouldn't need to see a counsellor anyway. But once the service is for everybody, including staff, they portray it differently. Now users of the service are less likely to be described as weird or weak: rather the opposite. Now getting support from a counsellor is on its way to becoming a normal, even an admirable thing for human beings in school to be doing and nothing to do with age, status or weakness.

Some schools insist on their new school counsellor seeing only students at first because the hierarchy doesn't yet trust the counsellor with distressed or disaffected members of staff. But as soon as the counsellor has earned some credibility in the staffroom, various members of staff quickly make themselves known. They stop the counsellor in the car park. They ask for advice about a student. They say that they're interested in how people become counsellors. They joke about having a 'chat' themselves sometime. Eventually, they ask to book a time 'to talk some things through'.

'But what about boundaries?' say purist counsellors, horrified. 'You can't see someone for counselling who's also your colleague!'

I disagree. It's perfectly possible to work with members of staff and for boundaries to be maintained outside the counselling room. Indeed, it's an important part of the therapeutic process, establishing counselling as *normal* – not furtive or shameful. I explain to staff (as I do to students) that 'When I see you outside the room in meetings or in the canteen or car park, I'll say hello as usual but I won't stop you and ask about the things we've talked about in here: not because I'm not interested or wondering, but because it wouldn't be fair to start that conversation when there are other people around, when you weren't expecting it and when there isn't time to talk properly.' The rules of engagement are clear, and my experience of colleagues away from the counselling room is often a hugely important part of our counselling relationship. In the privacy of the counselling room I may have been allowed to share a person's fears and vulnerabilities, but outside it I'm able to witness and appreciate their resourcefulness as they run assemblies, organise teams, confront difficult students and teach great lessons. The message is that there's no splitting: my colleagues are people who are fearful *and* competent, vulnerable *and* successful. And for their part, they might experience me as attentive and serious in the counselling room – a competent counsellor – while outside it I'm a hopeless jammer of photocopying machines, a person endlessly asking for help with his computer. Like them, I'm patient and impatient, competent and incompetent.

In schools, credibility is all, but credibility isn't earned by being perfect. As Chapter 2 describes, a new counsellor must bear the hostile projections of staff and students because the school will look to its new counsellor for answers when the going gets tough. Surely one good counselling session will turn around the behaviour of the most disruptive students? Counsellors feel the weight of these expectations: the baleful eyes of staff, the barely concealed disappointment.

This has to be borne. Counselling may eventually affect a person's behaviour. But never overnight. And never by itself. Counselling may be a crucial help but only ever a crucial *part* of what helps. Yet it's easy for counsellors to be seduced into believing that they alone can make a difference and then, when progress is inevitably slow (Louis Baker has been in yet another fight and been excluded yet again), it's tempting to speed things up by making and-so-you-see links: 'And so you see, the reason you don't get on with Mr Benson in History is because he reminds you of your step-father!' or 'You're angry because that's the way your father always expressed his feelings!' or 'You're struggling this year because you've lost your Maths teacher, Mrs Pandit, like you've lost so many other mother figures in your life!'

Offered in the name of 'insight', these may be perfectly sensible, accurate interpretations but, as with all interpretations, timing is everything. Under pressure to transform a student's behaviour, counsellors sometimes end up offering their interpretations prematurely, before the young person has had time to digest the feelings involved. Insight isn't the ultimate goal of therapy. We may understand the connections perfectly well; we may know the reasons why we do the things we do: these insights will make little difference to how we feel when so much of our behaviour will be driven by feelings and anxieties rather than by thoughts and insights. Jonathan Swift is alleged to have quipped, 'It is useless to attempt to reason a man out of what he was never reasoned into' (in Knowles 2009, p.784).

Frustrated by all this and desperate to make a difference, the counsellor determines to 'challenge' the student: 'It's not fair to take your feelings about your father out on your mother!' or 'Why have sex with so many people when you know that they don't love you?' or 'Picking fights with other people isn't right and you know it!'. These well-intentioned challenges make absolutely no difference; students are already hearing them from all sorts of other professionals.

I'm caricaturing. Few counsellors would resort to such clumsy admonitions. It's just that it's hard to resist the pressure to wave a magic wand when that's what the school seems to be expecting. It's hard to bear the school's obvious disappointment when its new counsellor turns out not to be a magician. It's hard to stay confident, knowing that a student's behaviour will be completely unaffected until something shifts internally and that internal shifts happen because of relationships which take time to develop. It's hard to be patient with all this, knowing that the quality of relationships in the school as a whole – relationships *outside* the counselling room – will influence any internal shifts as much as the work of the counsellor.

This book is about developing schools in which these relationships are eventually more warm-hearted and accepting of difference than they might otherwise be. It's a book about counselling becoming a normal part of school life: not something esoteric, weird or scary. It's a book about schools in which counsellors are never a breed apart but are linked in with everything else that's happening. If – as is sometimes said – a client is ready to finish counselling when she's internalised her counsellor ('In my head, I knew exactly what you'd say!'), then the counselling service will have done a good job when it's taken for granted in a school. Paradoxically, that will be when students and staff all pride themselves on their *own* counselling skills and are no longer rushing to the counsellor at the first sign of trouble.

Part One

THE CONTEXT

2
THE IDEA OF A COUNSELLOR

Schools recruit counsellors for a variety of reasons. The headteacher may have had a good experience of counselling in another school. Or a group of influential parents may have been lobbying the school about the need for counselling. Or the counsellor may have come as a free gift, offering to work for nothing... The official reasons why the counsellor has been recruited may vary but the unofficial reason won't: schools hope that a counsellor will transform the behaviour of the most difficult students. Like other vaunted professionals coming through the school gates for the first time, the counsellor represents the possibility – at last – of someone who'll make everything all right. This is the counsellor's passport through the gates, but also the counsellor's burden once inside them because plenty of other professionals will have been trying to make everything all right and trying for a very long time.

'It's good that you're here,' say the teachers, 'because we need all the help we can get. Some of our students, as I'm sure you know, can be quite...challenging!'

Trying to sound humble without sounding clueless, the counsellor says that she'll do her best.

'We've got a waiting list already,' says one of the teachers, Mrs Woolstencroft. 'We can get you started as soon as you're ready.'

What Mrs Woolstencroft doesn't say but might be expecting is that, like other pampered outsiders she's worked with, this counsellor will probably want to begin by cherry-picking a few mildly troubled students and will then want to go at a ridiculously slow pace with them.

'I'm happy to get started,' says the counsellor gamely, aware that the stakes are high and that credibility is all.

'Well I could get Sarah Smith for you after break,' says Mrs Woolstencroft, 'if you're sure that you want to get started?'

The counsellor agrees to see Sarah.

Mrs Woolstencroft looks doubtful. 'Would it help if I told you a bit about her? Needless to say, there are no parents on the scene and, as usual, the social workers are taking ages to sort out the mess. So in the meantime Sarah's out on the streets every night and getting into all sorts of trouble. We've got no idea where she's staying. She comes in to school but, unfortunately, has to stay in my office all day because some of the students and – to be honest – some of the staff are scared of her. Amazing, really, that she keeps coming in, but I suppose it must mean that we're doing something right!'

Dismayed, the counsellor listens, saying nothing.

'Anyway, I expect you'll have met plenty of youngsters like Sarah before,' says Mrs Woolstencroft. 'I'll find her and get her to see you after break. It's probably best if I don't tell her anything about you. I'll leave you to introduce yourself, okay?'

These situations have to be borne. The counsellor has to get started somewhere. Insisting that everything must be done on her terms will only fuel the resentment of teachers who feel that they have no control over their working environment so why should anyone else? In schools, credibility has to be earned the hard way. The counsellor may represent the hope that everything will be all right but also the fear that it won't be, that nothing will ever improve. So teachers welcome the counsellor because part of them hopes that she'll be wonderful while another part of them hopes that she'll fail miserably, proving that they alone understand young people, that they alone can make a difference and that they alone have the stamina to deal with the likes of Sarah Smith. *And* – what's more – deal with her without special training or a special room, without the luxuries of having Sarah on her own with no exams to pass, no uniform to fight over and no colleagues baying for disciplinary blood. In schools, counsellors are the objects of hope but also of envy and resentment (Halton 1994).

Students feel these things as powerfully as staff. The counsellor does indeed meet after break with Sarah Smith, a girl with a lifetime of broken attachments, a girl with a history of professionals coming into her life, all promising to understand, all promising to help. Many will have ended their relationship with her after six months – transferred to other placements, promoted to other jobs, 'I'm really sorry, Sarah!' they'll have said to her. 'You know it's not personal, don't you?' A counsellor has to stay in a school for several years to start enjoying the satisfactions of the role. Until then, the suspicions remain. Is this just another well-meaning professional, making a few brief relationships before moving on to something more glamorous? A school doesn't properly invest or believe in its counsellor until she's demonstrated some serious staying power.

The counsellor does her best, explaining who she is, careful not to raise Sarah's expectations unfairly.

Sarah listens with her best I've-heard-all-this-before expression. She tests the counsellor with some swearing. 'This school's shit! I hate the fucking teachers! Especially that bitch Woolstencroft! I've seen millions of counsellors! The only thing I like doing is getting out of my head!'

Again, the counsellor has to bear this, knowing that it's Sarah's understandable response to yet another sympathetic professional. To invest any hope in this person would be too painful. So Sarah doesn't. Instead, she reels off a disjointed selection of autobiographical fragments, getting the counsellor to feel as worthless and as foolish as she feels herself – struggling, as it were, to get out of her head. She ends the session by saying that she doesn't want to meet again.

The counsellor realises that she'll have to fight for the relationship. It's what Sarah probably wants but would never admit. It's also the counsellor's only way of assuring the school of her commitment: accepting the most difficult student and never giving up.

She makes another appointment with Sarah. 'Just in case you change your mind. If you forget, I'll come and find you.'

Sarah goes out, muttering.

Later in the day, Mrs Woolstencroft asks how the session went, adding quickly, 'I saw Sarah afterwards and she said she didn't want to meet with you again.'

The counsellor feels terrible and is *meant* to feel terrible. Ruth Woolstencroft might well be thinking but doesn't say, 'How dare you come into our school, helping people! We've been doing that for years! How dare you!' Part of her will be relieved that Sarah has given the new counsellor a hard time and, provided that the counsellor doesn't now capitulate, Ruth will be more kindly disposed towards her, reassured that her rival is neither omnipotent nor omniscient.

'People become real to us by frustrating us,' writes Phillips (2012, p.29). In the weeks ahead, Sarah will continue to make life as difficult as possible for the counsellor: forgetting appointments, clamming up, looking bored, walking out of sessions early, saying that there's no point in continuing... The counsellor will continue to be tested by Sarah, but also – implicitly – by the school. Writing about the role of the trouble-maker in institutions, Obholzer and Zagier Roberts (1994) argue that 'The unconscious suction of individuals into performing a function on behalf of others as well as themselves happens in all institutions' (p.131). It's as if Sarah tests the counsellor on behalf of the school as well as herself.

A counsellor's first job is to survive. That's the only thing that will give Ruth Woolstencroft and Sarah Smith any real hope when so many other professionals will have given up, saying that they've decided to refer Sarah on to some other agency. It could well be that Sarah is a wholly inappropriate referral for the counsellor because her life at the moment is too chaotic for her to make much use of counselling. This may be true but the counsellor has to play a long game, thinking not only about what's best for Sarah but also about the *meaning* of Sarah. Sarah may be representing all the school's chaos, yet somehow the counsellor has to keep thinking despite all that chaos. Ruth Woolstencroft may have presented the counsellor with a version of herself because Sarah may be how Ruth sometimes feels – angry, unwanted, unsupported, hopeless and yet still willing to attach to 'school' and to the hopeful possibilities it represents (Luxmoore 2008).

If Ruth and Sarah are combining to make the counsellor feel useless, there are other teachers and students who play an equally hostile game: idealising rather than demonising the new counsellor. Some students will claim that this new counsellor is fantastic and that their first session has been life-changing. Hearing this, their teachers will say how pleased they are, but they'll envy the newcomer her wonderfulness. They'll take an unconscious revenge on her by saying, 'Sarah loved it! She thinks you're the best – thank you so much! You're obviously the person we've all been waiting for!' but will make no secret of their disappointment when, next week, the illusion is shattered because the counsellor *hasn't* made everything miraculously better; she *hasn't* rescued everyone and so now it turns out that she's completely useless after all!

Hope and despair, idealisation and demonisation… These are all aspects of what Hewitt (2000) calls the 'institutional transference' to the new counsellor. Towards the end of her first week, the counsellor bumps into the headteacher.

'I've heard all about you!' he says. 'It sounds as if you're already making an impact!'

The counsellor is unsure whether to accept the praise or be deeply suspicious.

'Have you got a minute?' asks the headteacher. 'As you know, I wasn't here when you were appointed and it would be good to meet you properly…' He ushers the counsellor into his office.

Headteachers are vital. Male and female, they work extremely hard and their school (*their* school) means everything. It's personal. So criticising any aspect of the school can be a dangerous thing to do. Because of her own need to be needed, Ruth Woolstencroft may have made it difficult for the counsellor to work with Sarah Smith – rushing them into a relationship, setting them up to fail – but reporting any of this to the headteacher is unlikely to be well received. As yet, the counsellor has no credibility, whereas Ruth, for all her shortcomings, has probably served him loyally for years.

The headteacher knows perfectly well that *someone* has to engage with students like Sarah Smith every day and it can't be him. Without Ruth, he'd be stuck. So for an outsider to draw attention to Ruth's imperfections or to the imperfections of any of his staff is probably telling him what he already knows but what the counsellor hasn't earned the right to say. Headteachers may feel besieged and demonised, but fresh criticism still makes them resentful. They rarely get any praise, especially if they make a virtue of deflecting it immediately onto students and staff ('Well of course we've got a wonderful staff team here and our students are great!'). But however formidable or unconcerned they may appear to be, headteachers enjoy praise as much as any other human being.

Wisely, the counsellor says how impressed she's been with everyone's friendliness, with the look of the school, with the politeness of students. This is mainly true.

The headteacher looks pleased. 'We do our best,' he says. 'We're improving all the time but we know that there's still a long way to go.' He asks the counsellor how she sees things developing over the next few months.

The answer to this question is crucial because, for any counsellor in any school, a productive relationship with the headteacher is essential. Unless the counsellor intends to remain aloof and peripheral, the work that she'll be able to do will depend on the quality of this relationship. The headteacher will ultimately block things or make them possible, endorsing or undermining the counsellor, encouraging her participation in decision-making or keeping her at arm's length. Ultimately, the headteacher will decide whether or not the counsellor remains at the school.

'How do you see things developing over the next few months?'

It's an interview question because this is effectively an interview. The headteacher may have allowed others to make the appointment, but only because he knows that he'll make up his own mind once the counsellor starts work. He knows that he can always get rid of her by making her life impossible.

'How do you see things developing over the next few months?'

In beginning to answer the question, it's worth remembering that the headteacher and Ruth Woolstencroft will have their own passionate reasons for working with young people like Sarah Smith. Apart from going to work to earn money, they'll be powered by reasons that are personal and often unconscious, arising from their own adolescent experiences, their own experiences of authority, their own parenting, their own schooldays.

Counsellors are no different. I've met counsellors still hostile to teachers because of their own school experiences 25 years ago. Over-identified with young people, they make no secret of whose side they're on. Not surprisingly, teachers sense this and waste no time in making life difficult for the counsellor. I've met other counsellors trying to work in schools with no sense of what it's like to be an angry or frightened young person. They can't help seeing things always from an adult's point of view. Inevitably, young people pick up on this and vote with their feet.

The obvious conclusion is that counsellors like these are just not very good, needing more therapy themselves at the very least. Maybe so. But *all* counsellors will start work with strong feelings about school based on their own experiences. There'll be traps for everyone. For some, the idea of a counsellor will be of a rescuer. For others, a counsellor will be of a friend or advocate or good parent. I think it's important to avoid any fixed notions of what a counsellor in school will be: every therapy will need to be different. But the biggest trap of all will be in believing that what a counsellor does is completely different from what everyone else does.

'How do you see things developing over the next few months?'

For headteachers, the counsellor is a potential threat because students and staff will tell the counsellor things that they won't necessarily tell the headteacher. And they'll tell the counsellor *about* the headteacher. In that sense, the counsellor is the headteacher's love rival and, for some headteachers, this is too much to bear: they set about destroying their rival. But the counsellor is also a potential ally, a potential source of support, a potential collaborator. If the two people with arguably the loneliest jobs in the school can work together, all kinds of things become possible: insights and frustrations shared, schemes hatched, anxieties contained. The headteacher may know this or, never having worked with a counsellor before, may simply be intrigued, sensing possibilities.

'How do you see things developing over the next few months?'

Somehow, the counsellor has to sound authoritative but deferential, experienced but flexible, with ideas of her own but making no assumptions.

The headteacher listens. He'd quite like the chance to answer the question himself. And when it's his turn, he'll make it clear to the counsellor that, whilst he's in charge, he's happy to defer to what he imagines will be her particular skills. He'll say that he knows his school but that he's always open to new ideas...

They've begun their relationship, each needing to earn credibility in the eyes of the other, each needing the other, each with authority, although the headteacher ostensibly has all the power and the counsellor – for all her qualities and experience – none.

It's tough work, starting as a counsellor in a school. I know because I've started in several and have helped launch counselling initiatives in others. When things are difficult, it's tempting to blame the school, the unsatisfactory circumstances, the seemingly unappreciative staff. It's tempting to conclude that 'This school's just not ready for counselling!' or that 'They don't really want a counsellor!' In short, it's tempting to give up. But giving up never helps the school. Counsellors have to persist. Every practical difficulty, every professional slight will be an expression of institutional anxiety: anxiety developed over years. It won't be undone in a matter of weeks.

3
DEMYSTIFYING COUNSELLING

'So what exactly is it that you do?'

Lots of people in the staffroom have been wanting to ask that question and wanting to ask other questions as well... 'Are you a psychoanalyst? Can you read my mind? Are you interpreting everything I say? How does being a counsellor differ from being a tutor? Are you cleverer than us? Do you agree with the rest of the world that teachers are lazy, stupid and shallow? Are you the kind of person I might talk to myself one day? Would you be interested in me?'

I wonder how to reply... How to be authoritative but unthreatening, clear but unassuming? 'The beauty of my job is that I've got time to listen,' I say. 'I'm not rushed off my feet, having to teach one class after another. I've got the luxury of seeing one person at a time.'

Steve, my original questioner, asks, 'Do you have to have years of training to be a counsellor?'

'Of course you do!' say a couple of his colleagues, sitting nearby, laughing.

I tell them that I've trained for a long time and have also worked as a counsellor in other schools.

'Must be an interesting job,' says Steve. 'Bet you hear all sorts!'

I say yes, it's a privilege talking with people about the things that are going on in their lives.

'Must be hard to know what advice to give...'

'It's not usually advice that people are wanting,' I say. 'It's more the chance to talk about what's happening at home and what's happening with friends and what's happened in the past – all the things that get in the way of learning in school and feeling good about ourselves.'

Steve's gone quiet.

One of the other teachers picks up the questioning. 'And d'you find that many students *do* want to talk about those things? Upsetting things?'

I say that you'd be surprised at how much goes on in people's lives and how much young people have to bear.

'I don't think I'd be a very good counsellor then,' says this teacher, Xanthe. 'I had a girl last year who was taking drugs and cutting herself. Her father was in prison and her mother didn't seem to care what happened! I imagine that's the sort of thing you have to counsel people about, is it? I remember when she told me, I didn't know what to say!'

I tell her that it can be hard to know what to say sometimes.

'I don't think I could do your job!'

I say that being a counsellor is no more difficult than being a classroom teacher.

They seem pleased.

Counselling is concerned with demystifying our lives, with understanding our feelings and relationships and becoming better able to bear whatever life throws at us. So it follows that demystifying the processes of counselling itself is one of the first things that a school counsellor needs to do. For whatever reasons, psychotherapy has built a reputation for itself as difficult, dark, esoteric – the more esoteric the better if it keeps people out of the profession and maintains the illusion of therapist as all-seeing guru, thinking thoughts far too clever for ordinary mortals to comprehend. Such exclusivity is a shame if it means that the wonderful insights and learnings of psychotherapy are obscured. In a school, anything obscure or esoteric is deemed 'weird' and things weird deemed unworthy of consideration. Unless a counsellor can appear sufficiently normal and unless people can experience counselling as clear and understandable, no one will bother to invest in the counsellor and whatever it is that he or she has to offer will be wasted. So *normalising* the idea of counselling is a priority and a skill. And time spent doing this in the staffroom is as essential as time spent wandering the corridors, saying hello to people.

'Who's he?'

'That counsellor bloke.'

'What's his name?'

It's important, for example, to write regular reports for staff, not about what the individuals using the counselling service are saying, but about the service generally, reports which betray no confidentiality but which are nevertheless as transparent as possible, providing statistics, outlining the issues people typically talk about, analysing what's going well for the service and what's practically difficult, describing how things might develop in the future... This is all time spent demystifying counselling. McGinnis and Jenkins (2011) write: 'The counsellor is ultimately accountable to the young client but the nature of their work in schools also means that the counsellor will be accountable to the organisation employing them and the institution where they work' (p.13). This means that counsellors can't allow themselves to become mysterious and marginalised.

I introduce myself to an assembly of students. Members of staff stand at the sides of the hall, keeping an eye on the rows of students and listening intently themselves. I say that counselling is a chance to talk about things that are important – relationships, feelings, memories – things that sometimes get in the way of us living our lives. I say that I'm not *instead* of families or friends, teachers or all the other important people we talk to in our lives. I'm *as well as* those people: the difference is that I've got time to listen, whereas those other people are often busy. And I've got lots of special training to help me to be good at my job, I say. Sometimes it's useful to talk with someone who doesn't already know lots of things about you; someone who you're not going to be seeing every day. I don't really give advice, I tell them, because everyone is giving everyone else advice and normally that's the easy bit: the hard bit is actually *doing* the advice. I say that I'm better at trying to understand how stuff feels and sometimes that makes it easier to live with the relationships or the feelings or the memories. I describe the limits of the confidentiality I can offer and give specific examples to make this clear. I say that this confidentiality is exactly the same as that of teachers and other members of staff. Lastly, I explain to the students how they can make an appointment to see me and I remind them that the counselling service is for everybody. You may be quiet and hard-working; you may never get into trouble: this doesn't mean that your life will always be easy or that there won't be all sorts of difficult things that you're keeping to yourself.

In all this, my intention is to make counselling sound normal: a normal kind of support in addition to all the other kinds of support already available in school. A different kind of support, maybe, but no better or worse than other kinds of support and certainly not dark or esoteric.

My pitch is as much for the staff listening as for the students because, to begin with, most students will be meeting with me at the suggestion of a teacher. It's vital, therefore, that the teachers feel confident, vital that counselling isn't seen as strange or as a sign of weakness or as something reserved only for the most truculent or most obviously distressed students. Once counselling is established as normal – not shameful or furtive – then, in time, students will start referring themselves, a sure sign that things are changing with young people unafraid and able to organise support for themselves.

I repeat most of this when I meet with individuals for the first time, adding that – unfortunately – I don't do miracles. The young person smiles, as if this much was obvious. But it isn't. In schools, the idea of the counsellor as a magician (and, having failed as a magician, as a fraud) is never far away. Oddly, one of the most therapeutic things about counselling is when we're able to acknowledge that, by itself, counselling changes nothing. It doesn't heal relationships or bring people back from the dead. It doesn't change our parents or friends or enemies. In counselling, we can begin to understand and feel differently about these things, but the facts themselves can't be changed. In one sense, this is the great disappointment of counselling and counsellors but, in another sense, it's hugely reassuring to acknowledge that bad things really *do* happen; people *do* die; relationships *do* change and we're not missing a trick by sometimes feeling miserable about these things. At times, life really does suck.

Seventeen-year-old Marley has failed his English exam, yet again. 'It's so unfair!' he complains. 'And this time I worked really hard! But I mean, it's not my fault if my mum decides to walk out on us, is it? The night before the exam! And I'm supposed to be at home looking after my little sister all the time instead of revising because my mum's too fucked up! And then on the morning of the exam I come in and they send me to the wrong bloody room!'

I say that none of these things is fair. There's nothing else I can say. No sweet consolations.

'It's shit,' he says, 'and now I've failed and I've got to take the stupid exam *again!*' He pauses. Breathes. Shakes his head in frustration. Breathes again.

And smiles.

I'm back in the staffroom with Steve, Xanthe and some others, still intermittently curious about me and still not entirely convinced that I haven't got a magic wand hidden away in my bag.

'So what do you say,' asks Steve, 'when someone's mother's died or their parents have just split up? Presumably you've got to reassure them?'

I reply that I'd do exactly what he or Xanthe or any of the others would do. I'd listen, I wouldn't make false promises and I'd try to avoid platitudes. 'The most we can usually do for each other is to be there and help a person bear whatever it is that they're going through,' I say. 'Sometimes there's nothing to say. Nothing to do. Sometimes life's just shit!'

They laugh.

'I don't think I'd be able to leave it like that,' says Xanthe, unimpressed. 'I think I'd want to say something comforting at least.'

'Maybe,' I say, 'but if you think of the times in your life when things have been difficult, my guess is that what you needed most wasn't comfort so much as someone to listen to how it felt; someone not to be scared of your sadness or your anger; someone to be there and not run away.'

'That's what we do as tutors, though,' says Steve, 'or what we should be doing!'

I agree with him.

'So, are you saying that's all it is?'

'Well there's a bit more but that's the most important thing. That's what matters most. So if you see me running round in six months' time, acting like I'm the only person who can understand young people and like I'm the solution to everyone's problems, give me a good kicking and remind me of what I've just said!'

There are counsellors who make no secret of the fact that they're listening to terrible tales all day and shouldering everyone's burdens. Their message to the world is that they're indispensable and that their schools couldn't possibly manage without them because they alone understand. Like any cult of personality, this does no one any favours, encouraging a dependency and potentially disempowering hundreds of young people and adults perfectly capable of supporting each other and perfectly capable of doing so more confidently and skilfully with a little help from a counsellor. Counsellors can run training courses for staff; they can write about their work; they can train and manage teams of peer supporters... Above all, they can increase other people's confidence in themselves as listeners by modelling a transparency (counselling isn't a mystery), an inclusiveness (nor is it reserved for those who shout loudest) and a simple warm-heartedness as they move about the school.

They can also make a point of never panicking when everything seems to be going wrong. Davies (2012) describes the way in which human suffering was once upon a time seen as normal and noble whereas nowadays we expect to avoid suffering thanks to education, legislation, anti-depressants and a folder of rigorous health and safety policies. Given this, counsellors have to remind people that suffering and all the things that go wrong in life, while painful and regrettable, are normal and inevitable. Other people may panic but the counsellor won't. The next time he sits the English exam, Marley may fail again. And worse things will happen during the course of a typical school year – his mother may die of alcoholism, his sister may be taken to live elsewhere by the authorities – but whatever happens, Marley will cope, the counsellor will help him to cope and the school will cope.

In schools and in other organisations whose job is to care for people, there's usually an unspoken fear of scarcity (Smith and Berg 1987). Schools worry in public about not having enough staff to teach so many students; they worry about not having enough money to pay for everything. But their unspoken fear is of not having enough love: a fear that the needs of young people and their families will be so overwhelming that staff will simply run out of love and everything will then collapse. When members of staff complain about not having enough time to listen to individual students, I think that what they really mean is, 'If I did have enough time, I'm not sure that I'd be adequate to the task and I hate that feeling. It's impossible to love so many needy young people! I can't do it!'

I remember working in one school where a student's suicide brought this into focus. Suddenly, everyone was wondering whether they could have done more to prevent what had happened and whether they should be doing more now. Suddenly a clutch of students seemed like suicide risks and, for a while, they weren't allowed to go on school trips in case they 'did something'. Staff became especially anxious if one of these students was unsupervised or found to be missing from a lesson.

This anxiety was perfectly understandable and born of the realisation that – actually – any student could kill themselves at any time; there'd be nothing that a member of staff could do to stop it. So how could members of staff possibly love everyone enough to prevent another suicide? School counsellors have to live with this same fear of never having enough love for everyone, never mind hours in the day. How counsellors live with it potentially affects how other members of staff learn to live with it.

It's often said that – with uncanny accuracy – clients will always work on their counsellor's issue. So a counsellor with a dying mother will find that all his clients suddenly want to talk about bereavement.

A counsellor unable to have children will find that all her clients have fertility issues. In schools, students invariably pick up the anxieties of staff. If the school's budget is threatened and teachers are afraid of losing their jobs, then – as if by magic – the behaviour of students will obliquely express all sorts of anxieties about separation and loss. If a new headteacher is about to be appointed, students will be talking about step-parents more than usual.

Equally, staff pick up the anxieties of students. If students are afraid of the future and asking, in effect, 'What will become of me?', then staff will develop their own fears about the future. Steve has been saying hello to me enthusiastically ever since our earlier staffroom conversations and recently came on a training course I was running about anger. Now he makes an appointment to see me.

Sometimes a member of staff will come into my room, sit down and burst into tears. Sometimes, they'll come in and begin to speak confidently about whatever's troubling them. But more often than not they come in nervously like Steve. I show them where to sit. I start making tea or coffee and I talk about the latest goings-on at school, the things we have in common: the dreadful weather, the incident at lunchtime last week, the number of days left until the holidays, the latest rumours circulating about changes for next year. What this establishes is that we're in it together; we have a shared experience. We may have quite different roles in the school but we're colleagues and I'm not about to sit in judgement. This is important because – as with young people – members of staff are forever afraid of being shamed. Indeed, this fear will probably have prevented Steve from coming to see me sooner.

'I've been thinking of coming to talk to you for a while but never got round to it,' he begins. 'And I was thinking this morning about what I wanted to talk about and I'm not sure, really. I think I just want a chat!'

I say that's fine and ask how things have been lately.

'Okay, really,' he hesitates. 'Same as ever... I think maybe that's the problem. I just seem to be carrying on with things and that's fine but I suppose I wonder sometimes whether that's enough or whether I should be doing more...'

He tells me about his work in school, about the pleasures and frustrations of the job, the personalities involved, the politics. It's been his only job since leaving university and he's been doing it now for twelve years. Twelve years at the same school. During that time, he's been promoted, but not dramatically. He's a middle manger: one of the thousands of people who make schools tick, implementing new government initiatives, responding to the changing emphases of different headteachers, dealing with the daily round of unexpected incidents, feeling content in many ways but taken for granted in others.

I ask if he has a family.

'Do you mean parents? I've got my mum and dad and two brothers. They're all still alive.'

I ask what they're like.

'They're fine. One of my brothers is quite high-flying in London. He's a civil servant. The other lives in Australia with his wife. He's a computer geek but, to be honest, I think he spends most of his time on the beach! They're both heavily into surfing.'

I ask Steve if he has a partner.

He makes a face, avoiding my eye. 'Not at the moment,' he says, looking away. 'I wouldn't mind. In fact, to be honest, I wouldn't mind at all but, you know, I just haven't met anyone.' He looks back at me anxiously.

'It must be hard when you're working all the time...'

'You can say that again!'

'Do you ever think of moving to another school?'

'All the time! This is the only school I've taught in. I'm 35. I might be here for the rest of my life!'

The anxiety of being single is a preoccupation for many younger teachers. Some come into the profession with established partners; others meet people when they're still in their twenties; others like Steve get stuck, wondering if their number will ever come up and, if not, what they should do about it. In every social situation, they're confronted by couples and, every day at work, they overhear students talking about sex, sex, sex: the thing that teachers are supposed to have risen above, as if sex ceases to be an issue once you're a teacher.

'Have you been out with people yourself, Steve?'

'A few, but nothing serious.'

What he probably means is no, nobody. And this is potentially very shaming for a 35-year-old man, a successful teacher, a university graduate responsible for other people's children: a virgin, possibly, who goes home at night and heats up another ready-meal for one.

'I've tried a bit of speed-dating,' he says, 'but nothing so far!'

For one man to admit this to another man is a leap of faith. So much remains unspoken. Steve may be gay; he may be straight. He may use internet porn; he may be one of the many men and women for whom hard work and tiredness block out other issues. Steve can involve himself in all sorts of school business; he can arrive early every morning and leave late every evening – good old Steve – but underneath all that...

We talk about what it would be like to apply for other jobs – the pros and cons, the knowns and unknowns. We're simply opening up the subject as a practical possibility and I'm hoping that talking with me about it makes the idea of leaving slightly less of a taboo. I remember the high proportion of teachers attending a support group I once set up who were thinking of leaving that particular school. It was as if joining the group provided them with a transitional kind of experience, giving them permission to try out a different kind of conversation. If he and I keep meeting, our sessions may serve the same purpose for Steve.

Whatever it is that members of staff come to discuss – their fury at some perceived slight, their resentment of authority, their loss of professional impetus, their desire for something more from life or their questioning of life's purpose – it's important that my colleagues walk out at the end of the session feeling respected and valued: often the very things that they complain of *not* feeling. I try to ensure that they never walk out feeling infantilised. This means that I work on *not* becoming the parent figure in the relationship. During the session I'll have made my comments – perhaps an insight here or a good question there, perhaps a sharing of experience – but I'll have remained a colleague: no better or cleverer or wiser than the professional brave enough to make this appointment and begin to do what – for someone like Steve – is a very unusual thing: talking about himself, his life, his parents and childhood, his fears and motivations.

He and I agree to meet again in a month and see where he's got to with his thinking. I explain that, when I see him around in the meantime, I'll say hello as usual but won't stop him in the corridor or staffroom to ask questions. 'Not because I'm not wondering,' I say, 'but because it wouldn't be fair to start talking about these things with other people around, when you weren't expecting it and without time to talk properly.'

He nods, understanding.

'So I'll wait until we meet again in a month and then we can see how things have been…'

The rules of engagement clear, he gets up to go. 'Thanks for the coffee…' He hesitates at the door. 'I never thought I'd say this but it wasn't as bad as I thought it would be, talking to you!'

I follow him out of the room, cursing the fact that it's raining and we're both about to get wet.

4 PRACTICAL RULES

Teachers recognise the syndrome. After a brief honeymoon period (sometimes weeks, sometimes minutes), there's a boundary challenge. Someone tests the rules and everyone's watching to see what will happen next. Will the teacher hold the line? Will she insist on the rules, even if that means becoming Public Enemy Number One ('We thought you were all right, Miss! We didn't realise that you were like *this!*') because only once the rules are firmly established and taken for granted can her students feel safe. Only then can the real work begin.

It's the same with counselling. A new counsellor may have spent time wandering benevolently down school corridors getting to know people, but before long the challenges start to arrive. She arrives in the morning to find that a French teacher is using the counselling room for an oral exam, while a student is waiting outside the room, wanting to be seen at short notice because of a crisis at home. An agitated teacher stops her in the corridor to ask if counselling sessions can be shortened to fit in extra students. A student bursts into tears at the end of a difficult session, saying that she can't face leaving the room and then, at break time, the deputy headteacher says, 'I know you're full but could you possibly fit in one more?'

Another student is asking if her best friend can accompany her to a session that afternoon, and later, one of the receptionists knocks on the door of the counselling room, wanting to take the student inside off for an urgent meeting somewhere else. To make matters worse, a group of boys have started banging on the counselling room door whenever they go past.

Of course there's a story behind each of these incidents; they're often ways in which people are communicating obliquely with the counsellor. The French teacher may have her own unconscious reasons for trying to sabotage the counsellor's work; the annoying group of boys banging on the door may be curious to meet the new counsellor but have no other way of getting her attention. Yet these are all boundary challenges to which the counsellor must respond. Just like a classroom teacher, she must be firm and seen to be firm, even when that means going from being idealised Universal Provider to demonised Crap Counsellor. And, of course, there's never a right answer: schools value firmness but also value flexibility.

Crisis counselling is the thin end of the wedge. Once a counsellor starts having impromptu sessions precipitated by crises, then there's no holding back the tide. Teachers no longer know where they stand with students rushing out of their lessons in a rage or in tears, demanding to see the counsellor. There's the same problem with 'open' sessions at lunchtimes for 'anyone wanting to pop in', sessions effectively for people wanting to queue-jump, bypassing the system of formal appointments, breaking the rules.

A good school counselling service needs to be there for everybody, regardless of how loudly one particular person happens to be shouting. There are schools where the only way to get attention is to behave badly – to shout loudly, in effect. Students appear, demanding to be seen because of a crisis. But once they've succeeded and an ad hoc culture is established, the chances vanish of quieter, unassuming students ever getting an appointment.

I remember supervising a school counsellor who began his new job anticipating a rush of referrals. Wanting to prioritise, he devised a referral form for staff to fill in with the details of individual students, asking staff to rate each student's need as 'low', 'average' or 'urgent'. Not surprisingly, every referral form came back as 'urgent'!

Referral forms tend to be defensive. In effect, they're ways of slowing everything down, ways of saying no (or not yet) without having to say it in person. By bureaucratising the need, the counsellor tries to deal with the fear of being overwhelmed. Menzies Lyth (1988) famously describes nurses defending themselves against their feelings about dying patients by making their interactions with these patients as formal and mechanical as possible. In huge organisations and in acute mental health settings, referral forms may be practically and clinically necessary, but in schools full of students demanding to be seen now or wanting to prolong sessions, in schools where a counsellor's boundaries will always tested by deputy headteachers wanting to 'fit in one more', there are times when the counsellor has to say no and say it in person.

'But I *need* to see you!' says one student. 'It's all gone wrong at home and my mum's probably going to kick me out tonight!'

'I can't stop crying!' says another student. 'My whole life's falling apart. You're the only person I can talk to! Please let me stay a bit longer! I beg you!'

'It would be really helpful,' says the deputy headteacher, 'if you could just squeeze another one in… Of all the students in this school, she's the one we're most concerned about and I'm afraid that you're our last hope!'

We say no to young people and worry that we're not being compassionate. We say no to staff and worry that we're being lazy or inflexible. The need is always urgent, the situation always desperate.

'I don't suppose there's any chance of you seeing Matthew Waller?'

'I'm sorry but I'm completely full at the moment.'

'So, no chance then?'

'I'm afraid not.'

'He just needs someone to talk to and we don't have your expertise. Things at home have got much worse and we're really worried about him.'

'That sounds really difficult. I'm sorry.'

'No, no, it's fine. You can only see so many people, I realise that. I suppose we'll just have to think of something else, although, at this moment, I can't think what!'

The guilt is heavy. There's a temptation to scream, 'Don't you realise how hard I'm already working! Just because I don't go round bleating to everyone about it doesn't mean I'm not stretched to breaking point!' It's true that some counsellors are unduly precious with their time, spending almost as long writing up notes as they spend seeing clients, but I find myself reminding the counsellors I supervise (who are not precious about their time) that *you can only do what you can do*. Of course bad things might happen at any time and, of course, if any child or young person is in serious danger, you'll act. But most of the time there's nothing to do. People survive. They have to. It's just that they get frightened, and when they get frightened, they panic and regress, wanting the Universal Provider to make everything all right. Young people are good at getting staff to feel their panic, and some members of staff will pass on that panic to the counsellor at the first opportunity. So it may be hard for counsellors to say no, but it's a practical necessity and, in any case, a busy counsellor will almost certainly have no appointments free until the end of the following week.

In the long run, it's the job of the counsellor to help develop a school in which rules are inevitable, disappointments aren't tragedies and we get on with our lives even when, as young people say, 'shit happens'. Counselling can't make everything all right. It'll make its special contribution but that contribution will only ever be as *part* of what goes on in school. The counsellor will be one of many people offering support – never the only person. 'You can only do what you can do' sounds like a statement of the obvious, but it can be hard to live with one's limitations, unable to rescue people and situations. Sometimes counselling sessions have to end bleakly with an acknowledgement that things are difficult, unfair and muddled. The counsellor can feel useless, sending a young person back into the world without having Solved It. But sometimes the young person simply feels better for knowing that the counsellor is aware of what's happening and isn't offering false optimism. After sessions that seem particularly bleak with the counsellor feeling particularly useless, there are young people who come back the following week reporting that things have moved on and that the previous session was really helpful, while after sessions seemingly full of insight and connection, there are young people who come back reporting that everything has got much worse!

Like referral forms, 'assessments' are assumed to be part of a counsellor's formal repertoire but are usually inappropriate in a school. For young people, there are three problems with assessments. The first is the problem of being implicitly compared. If they're going to talk, young people want to get on with it, whereas being 'assessed' sounds like having to take an exam first. 'What's the point of this exam?' they might understandably wonder. 'What am I being tested on? What are the right answers? If this is about whether or not I can start counselling, then how much am I supposed to tell the counsellor? Am I supposed to sound suicidal? How do I know if my problems are important? Will the counsellor realise if I don't tell her everything?'

The second problem is that assessments are (or should be) mutual, whereas in a school, the chances of a young person ever feeling able to reject the counsellor on offer are slim to non-existent.

'Would you like to ask me any questions?' says the counsellor at the end of the assessment meeting.

'How should I know?' thinks the young person. 'What football team do you support?'

The third problem with assessments in schools is that telling one's story – however briefly – involves attaching to the person listening: investing and trusting, hoping to be understood and liked by that person (Holmes 2001). So for a young person to be 'assessed' by one counsellor and then denied counselling or passed on to another person for counselling repeats the bad experience of attachment that many young people have already had in their lives. And if the person doing the 'assessment' is going to be the young person's counsellor anyway, then why bother with a formal process called 'assessment'? Why not just get on with the counselling? Assessment should be an intrinsic part of what goes on in all counselling sessions anyway: 'What's important here? What's important but unspoken? Is now the right time to ask that question? Where does this session need to go?' Therapeutic priorities will always be emerging with the counsellor always weighing things up, developing a working hypothesis about what's needed from one session to the next.

Similarly, seeing young people for a fixed number of sessions may be a practical necessity in some contexts but makes no emotionally healthy sense to most young people. 'Am I a six-session person or a 16-session person? If I'm a six-session person and I take an overdose, will I become a 16-session person? I'm coming to the end of six sessions and I still haven't told my counsellor some of the most important things!' In schools, the need will always be great; there will always be a waiting list with the attendant anxieties of a waiting list. 'Assessment' doesn't make those anxieties go away. There are young people for whom the immediate crisis that brought them to counselling passes but who still need to keep coming in order to assure themselves that they still matter and are still interesting, even without a crisis. Therapeutically, this is very important. It's easy to assume that because a person's stories are no longer packed with emotion, the need for counselling must have ended, whereas, in fact, the need has simply changed. The experience of still mattering is profound: mattering without cuts or rage or tears or exclusions.

As I've said, there will always be a waiting list but what can change is a school's confidence in living with its anxieties about that list and in meeting the needs of the students on it. To help with this, a counsellor needs to be paying attention to the bigger picture. 'How can I help other members of staff feel more confident about supporting distressed young people themselves?'

On the courses I run for staff and in the conversations we have, there's a very simple message: 'You can be helpful just by trying to understand, especially by trying to understand how a young person is feeling. That alone will make a young person's life feel more bearable and less lonely.' On these training courses, we may busy ourselves with all sorts of practical listening exercises; we may discuss all sorts of theories of child and neurological development; we may identify all sorts of unconscious communications and defence mechanisms, all of which are very interesting. But nothing matters as much as the experience of one human being trying to understand another: trying and sometimes failing and trying again. 'That's what young people value,' I tell my colleagues. 'Young people don't care whether they've internalised a split-off part-object which they're now projecting as an unconscious, envious attack. They care whether or not the person listening understands what their life feels like. And understanding what another person's life feels like isn't always simple because our need to make everything all right can cause us to speed up or to stop listening; our own experiences can get in the way of understanding another person's. And that's where I can help. When you're stuck with a particular student, you and I can meet separately and try to untangle things because, at the end of the day, *you're* the adult the young person knows and trusts and wants to talk with; *you're* the person in whom he or she has chosen to confide. So don't run away!'

Lindsay says, 'I didn't know what to say. He stayed behind at the end of the lesson and was talking about his father shouting at his mother and how he heard it going on downstairs and I couldn't think of anything to say. I felt terrible!'

I ask what the boy might have been needing from her.

'Someone to listen? Someone to give advice?'

'What advice could you have given?'

'I don't know. That's why I've come to see you.'

'There probably wasn't much advice worth giving. My guess is that he got what he needed.'

'What?'

'Someone to listen and understand. Someone who clearly likes him and knows what a horrible situation he's in.'

'But that's not enough, is it!'

'It's usually as much as any of us can offer, Lindsay. It may not feel like much but it's a lot. He's lucky to have you.'

She looks unconvinced but less panicky than when she started telling me the story. All I'm doing is trying to understand *her* frustration, *her* feeling of uselessness, just as she's been trying to understand the boy's frustration and feeling of uselessness; I'm trying to help her bear those feelings without panicking or immediately referring this boy on to a counsellor he's never met before, the implication being that his life is too difficult for an 'ordinary' person like Lindsay to bear. Ultimately, it will be Lindsay's ordinariness that helps the boy, reminding him that life has to be lived without the benefit of magicians and that no single piece of wisdom will ever transform our lives.

5
THERAPISTS ADAPTING

How best to be with a young person in a counselling relationship? Counsellors on training courses practise listening to a partner without saying anything and, afterwards, describe what the exercise was like. Easy, say some: listening without saying anything gave me time to think. Impossible, say others: I was bursting with things to say. Those doing the talking also report their experiences. Not being interrupted was a luxury, say some; getting no response was horrible, say others. As a group, we conclude that there are some young people who need counsellors to keep quiet and let them talk while other young people need them to be much more directive, shaping the conversation.

So far, so straightforward. But it's worth wondering about the meaning of silence and the meaning of talk for young people. If silence is an original, pre-verbal, merged state between a mother and child, I wonder how far talk is the means by which they separate? They may start by imitating each other's sounds but, after a while, they learn to make different sounds and say different things to each other. Before long, they're starting to misunderstand each other and in a few years' time will be screaming, 'You don't know anything about my life!', their separation now complete, full of talk where once there was only silence.

I wonder how far returning to silence – refusing to speak – is sometimes a way of refusing to be separate? I wonder how much it expresses a longing to recapture an original, merged relationship with the world? For some young people, the silence they experienced as babies, held in the gaze of an attuned mother, will have felt blissfully safe, while for others *without* that experience of attunement, silence will have felt dangerously unsafe. So there are young people who, years later, will happily retreat to the safety of silence while others will be doing anything they can to avoid it: talking, texting, talking, texting, talking... For some, silence will be a defence against separation while, for others, talking will be a defence against the terrifying loneliness of silence.

With those young people who remain silent, there are dilemmas about what to do next. Does the young person need me to initiate some conversation? Or do I need to stay silent for longer? Should I ask something simple like 'What are you feeling?' or should I talk at length myself in the hope that the young person will eventually join in? At the moment, what exactly does this young person most need from me? With those young people who talk unceasingly, there are different dilemmas. Should I interrupt? How much is this young person's talk a blissful release and how much is it a frantic defence? How much is it helping and how much is it hindering our relationship?

An ability and willingness to talk will vary from person to person, with counsellors needing to adapt all the time. I've supervised some psychodynamically trained counsellors who begin their work with young people by deliberately saying very little, intent on spotting transference and counter-transference issues regardless of the young person's need to be silent or to talk. The zeal with which they do this comes from trainings where transference is the key to everything and the assumption of the training organisation is that clients will be consenting adults, able and happy to play by the rules of prolonged silences, able and happy to use a 'blank-screen' counsellor proffering enigmatically phrased interpretations over the course of months – if not years – of therapy.

The damaging neurological and emotional effects of an expressionless face on a child are well documented (Gerhardt 2004) and so it takes a very secure relationship for a young person to make use of pithy interpretations offered by a 'blank-screen' face. Adults make a more informed decision to sign up for counselling than young people, who are usually ambivalent and don't play by these rules. Instead, young people are looking for relationships in which there's give and take. Knox (2011) writes that:

> ...change in therapy crucially depends on the affect regulation that gradually develops from relational interaction; the emotional regulation offered by the relationship creates the conditions necessary for the neural development in the orbitofrontal cortex and other areas, on which affect regulation depends. (p.168)

So, rather than offering pithy interpretations, the counsellor's skill lies in thinking the thoughts, noticing what may be going on interpersonally but *not* making an overt interpretation. Of course, there'll be transference and counter-transference processes at play in any human relationship, but because young people are *young*, a much greater power imbalance exists in the counselling room than exists in most adult-to-adult counselling relationships. In a school, the counsellor comes with more life experience, with institutional authority conferred, with a more sophisticated ability to articulate thoughts and feelings. Sitting opposite, young people are instinctively defensive. Their defences may look fierce and determined but often they're brittle underneath and easily swept aside by a counsellor's interpretations. Horne (2006) writes that with adolescents '...one has to be careful to avoid humiliating them with one's interpretations – or using the interpretation as a weapon with which to hit back' (p.234).

Of greater value is the counsellor's *interest* in a young person's defence (however pernicious it may be), understanding it as having made complete sense to the young person at the time and as having seemed to be the obvious way of behaving in the circumstances. 'Feeling understood is a self-consolidating experience,' write Ornstein and Ornstein (1994, p.993). Only once a defence is properly understood can its owner ever begin to amend or change it (Pine 1985).

'So you hit him because he was annoying you...'

'Yeah.'

'And when you're annoyed, it feels bad...'

'Yeah!'

'Frustrating and embarrassing...'

'In a way.'

'So you hit him to stop feeling like that...'

'Yeah!'

We offer interpretations as helpful insights and yet, as I said in Chapter 1, insight isn't necessarily the goal of counselling with young people. There's a place for insight, but young people can have all the insight in the world: it won't necessarily affect their behaviour when, more often than not, their feeling will get in the way of their thinking. Interpretations can be subtly mutative but the skill lies in the ways in which the interpretations are presented. Transference and counter-transference interpretations, especially here-and-now interpretations of what's going on between the two people in the counselling room, are difficult for most young people to use, especially in the rough-and-tumble, pragmatic world of school where the purity of a more analytic counselling relationship is forever compromised by accidental meetings in the corridor and by all the other ways in which what happens in the counselling room overlaps with what happens outside it. In his critique of traditional psychoanalysis, Lomas (1987) points out that 'it is good to be appropriately rigorous, cautious and restrained. The mistake is to raise these commonsense measures to a rule or dogma that can have harmful consequences for the relationship...' (p.38). Therapists must first learn the analytic rules, he implies, in order then to depart *knowingly* from them in the interests of a more authentic, spontaneous relationship between equals.

I remember supervising a volunteer counsellor in the school where I worked. We'd interviewed and appointed her because, apart from being theoretically clear and perceptive about young people, we thought she was warm-hearted and that young people would like her.

She began work. I told her that there are two aims in any first session with a young person. The first is to write down some sort of family tree during or – more probably – after the session in order to think about the likely source of the young person's difficulties. The second and more important aim is to make enough of a relationship for the young person to come back the following week.

The young people she saw didn't come back. At the end of their first sessions, they told her that they felt better now, that they didn't need to come back and that it had all been very helpful. Thank you and goodbye.

I was curious. Together, we thought about each person's presenting and underlying difficulties. We wondered whether their stories were somehow connected with their decision to end counselling prematurely. Were they avoiding attachment? Nervous about intimacy? Were they determined not to be helped in order to maintain some entrenched belief about themselves? It didn't make sense. Most young people are keen to continue meeting beyond two, four or six sessions. Something was going wrong.

I asked about a particular boy.

'He didn't want to talk.'

'So what did you say?'

'Nothing. I waited for him to speak.'

'And he didn't say anything?'

'No. It felt really awkward. Really uncomfortable. I felt like I was his mother or something, trying to get him to talk. He was determined not talk to me.'

It became clear that this warm-hearted counsellor was going into the room and turning herself into an aloof, unyielding taskmistress in the belief that this was what was expected of her: you sit in a chair looking pensive and wait for the young person to speak and when he can't – because it feels too embarrassing or weird – you stare at him meaningfully and wait.

Fortunately, there were plenty of other young people on the waiting list. She changed her approach, setting out to be warmer, more proactive, more *herself* and – unsurprisingly – her new clients stayed. Moreover, she found herself enjoying their company and starting to enjoy the work. She still thought hard about what might be unsaid between them, what might be going on unconsciously, but now she was doing this at the same time as being personable, encouraging and pleased to see them.

I remember another volunteer counsellor, the graduate of a person-centred training, who also lost her clients, although it took them slightly longer to come up with their excuses. Like the psychodynamic volunteer, this counsellor stuck rigidly to what she'd understood from her training, following the young person's lead, trusting the young person to know best, endlessly reflecting back whatever the young person said. In short, she was as non-directive as possible in the belief that this would go down well with young people who'd be fed up with being bossed about by adults and who'd be wanting time to talk without interruption.

As an approach, it didn't go down well. The young people she saw might well have been fed up with the bossiness of adults but wanted something more robust from their counsellor, something less passive, more *normal*: someone able to respond with comments, asides, jokes, ideas of her own. In short, they wanted a relationship, a dialogue, rather than what amounted to a monologue performed under the endlessly accepting gaze of this well-meaning counsellor.

Applying a strictly psychodynamic or strictly person-centred method in counselling with shy, truculent, embarrassed, fearful young people doesn't work. The theory behind each of these methods is full of riches but, for young people, the style seems just too 'weird' when practised inflexibly. Young people need something much more interactive. Fonagy *et al.* (2004) describe the way in which a baby develops a sense of self out of an attuned, mirroring, reflective experience of its mother. By extension, young people will only be able to reflect on themselves in the manner and to the extent that they've been reflected on by others. So if the parental mirror they look at seems harsh and uninterested, a blank screen, the danger is that they come to view themselves harshly and as of little interest. If the mirror is passive and insubstantial, then they struggle to develop a clear sense of who they are. Reflecting has to be a two-way process involving interaction, exchange, mutuality, playfulness, a call and a response. Typically, a teacher says to the misbehaving student, 'I want you to spend time reflecting on your actions!' and yet this is precisely what the student has never learned to do. He can't reflect on himself because no one has ever reflected with him. A young person might well enter a counselling room for the first time, expressionless, monosyllabic, with no confidence in parent figures but needing what Alvarez (1992) calls an 'enlivening object'. Little by little, session by session, the counsellor begins to coax a response from the young person who begins to see himself reflected in the interested, animated face opposite, recognising himself in her recognition.

Hurry (1998) describes the therapist working in this way as a 'developmental object'. Of course there'll be transference and counter-transference processes, she argues, but the therapist's aim is to create a relationship out of which a young person can develop in ways that haven't previously been possible. There'll be elements of a parent–child relationship but the power in the relationship will ebb and flow. Through an essentially playful relationship, the young person will start to develop a sense of agency (Knox 2011), practising a repertoire of interactions with the therapist, trying out undeveloped social roles. Key therapeutic moments will emerge, not from cool interpretation, but from warm understanding, improvisation and mutual interest.

There's considerable skill in this approach: thinking analytically while behaving normally, assessing and responding to the therapeutic need while enjoying the relationship, going at an appropriate pace, steering the conversation towards the places it needs to go while remaining sensitive to the young person's defences and especially to the dangers of shaming. Winnicott's (1965) idea of 'intermediate space' or 'space between' is helpful, with his analogy of the mother-therapist containing the child's play, making it safe while allowing the child more and more space in which to explore and take risks. Eventually, the child develops the capacity to be alone, able to think about itself, look after and play by itself, having internalised enough of this early maternal experience.

In schools, this 'intermediate space' or 'space between' is a physical as well as a psychological space because counsellors are bound to see and meet young people in contexts other than the counselling room. There are therapeutic opportunities in corridors, classrooms and canteens, therefore: opportunities to play in this space between the world of the counselling room and the world of the corridor. Some young people are ready for this. We stop in the corridor and talk. We don't talk about the things we talked about last week in counselling. Instead, we talk about the price of canteen doughnuts, someone's new hair-do, the football results last night… Other young people aren't ready. Saying hello in the corridor would be intrusive, so we don't. Developmentally, they're keeping their counselling selves and their corridor selves separate for the time being.

In the corridor, I meet the teacher of a boy I've been seeing for the past few weeks.

'How are you getting on with him?' asks the teacher. 'Is there anything I should know?'

Most teachers understand about the confidentiality of counselling without having to be told. Even so, it's frustrating for conscientious teachers working day-to-day with a young person, caring about him, dealing with his ups and downs without necessarily being told the whole story (Heller 2000). It's easy to feel resentful and shut out by a counsellor behaving as if she's the only person who matters in a young person's life. So, despite knowing all about confidentiality, it's tempting to ask, 'How are you getting on with him? Is there anything I should know?' Often, it's a way of saying, 'Don't forget that I know him too! I know lots of things about him and, what's more, I've known him for a lot longer than you have. I might have interesting things to say about him!'

Somehow I have to field these questions without betraying the young person's confidentiality. At the same time, I have to make it clear that I value the teacher's role as another professional in the life of the young person.

'Of course,' I say, 'he's in your tutor group! You must know him well…'

'I've been his tutor for the last couple of years and I've taught him as well.'

'What's that been like?'

'Well, we've had our moments! He's a good guy,' says the teacher, 'just gets into too much trouble. But that's not surprising when you've had the life he's had!'

I nod.

'If you ask me,' says the teacher, 'his parents have got a lot to answer for. If they'd had proper boundaries from the beginning, we wouldn't be in this situation.'

Again, I nod in agreement.

'Out of interest,' asks the teacher, 'has he said anything about his mother? I wouldn't normally ask. It's just that I tried to phone her last week and the phone was dead. I don't suppose he's mentioned anything? Or does he talk mostly about school?'

'Most students end up talking about their home lives,' I say. 'We're the same when it comes to counselling. We always end up talking about our mothers and fathers and our lives at home.'

Often this is enough and the teacher backs off, pleased to have been taken seriously, respected as a fellow professional.

But this particular teacher persists. 'So, has he mentioned anything?'

'I'm sure he hasn't told me anything that he hasn't told you.'

'Nothing about his mother…?'

'Well, like I say, all young people talk about their parents. Obviously, like you, I keep whatever I hear confidential.'

By now, most teachers will have retreated.

'Oh, I wasn't asking for secrets!' says the teacher. 'I know that counselling's confidential. I was just wondering if he'd mentioned anything about his mother in the last week or so?'

If the young person *hasn't* mentioned his mother, I'm inclined to say so, although the danger of this is that some occasional fool might go back to the young person and say, 'I hear that you haven't mentioned your mother in counselling recently!' But if the boy *has* mentioned her – in fact, if he *specifically* mentioned the fact that his mother doesn't have a phone because she dropped it into the canal when she was drunk and said to her son that 'If that idiot tutor from school rings, tell him to fuck off!' then I'm left with no option…

'As I say, our conversations are confidential.'

This is the final rebuff, to be used only when all other possibilities are exhausted and there's no kinder, subtler way of telling a teacher to back off.

There's another kind of potentially creative 'intermediate space' or 'space between'. The unwritten rule is that counsellors don't disclose anything about themselves to their clients. Most adult clients can understand this and work with it but, for young people, not being allowed to know anything about the person who wants to know all about you is just plain weird. With young people, a counsellor's skill is in making an artificial situation seem as normal as possible, and in normal relationships there's give-and-take. So for a young person to ask politely 'Have you got children?' and be answered with a question rather than an answer, 'I'm wondering if it's important for you whether or not I have children?' or with the comment 'It's interesting that this matters so much to you...' is disconcerting. Even worse is the clumsy, admonishing, 'I think we're here to discuss you, not me!'

For many young people, responses like these are reminders of other inaccessible, withholding parent figures in their lives, the same ones that they were probably hoping to talk about. Getting these responses to perfectly innocent questions feels like getting counselling wrong, like trying to have a normal relationship but being made to feel foolish. As Lomas (1987) writes: 'The therapist cannot readily expect the patient to take a risk from which he himself holds back...' (p.172). Of course there'll be elements of transference behind the young person's curiosity; there'll be unspoken questions like 'Do you care about your other children more than me?' or 'Will I be able to have you to myself?' and there'll also be other, more straightforward, curiosities such as 'Are you gay or straight? Are you divorced? Do you know anything about children?' A counsellor can make a mental note of these things while answering the question as straightforwardly as possible.

I'm not suggesting that counsellors should start telling their life stories to young people – young people know perfectly well that this isn't the purpose of counselling – but given the inherent power imbalance in the relationship, an ability to normalise the situation is crucial. 'If I'm going to tell you all about me,' a young person might say, 'then I want to know *something* about you!' This seems perfectly reasonable. If abiding by counselling rules that forbid therapist self-disclosure means that young people don't come back for more sessions, then the rules have to be adapted. As long as counsellors think about *why* they're sharing information about themselves, as long as that information is for the young person's benefit and not because the counsellor is so moved that he can't hold on to his story any longer, then it makes sense to disclose things from time to time. Knox (2011) draws on the work of Beebe *et al.* (2010) to show that turn-taking behaviour between a parent and baby is the foundation of a child's sense of agency. How strange and developmentally unhelpful for a young person, therefore, if he or she takes a turn and gets no response from the counsellor.

I remember meeting with Catherine for the first time. She was the eldest of four children and her mother was just about to have a fifth child. She claimed to be excited about this but looked extremely glum. I decided to tell her about the time when, as the eldest of four children myself, I found out that my mother was having a fifth child. I told her that I'd said all the right things at the time about being pleased and excited but had cried in bed at night.

Catherine yelped with delight, jumped up and gave me a high-five hand-slap. 'That's it! That's exactly what I think!' she said, sitting back down again. 'I'm happy but not really. Well, I *am* happy for the baby and I'll be nice to it, but I know that nobody's going to take any notice of me once it's born!'

We went on to talk about her mixed feelings, about the conflict between responsible-14-year-old Catherine and crying-baby-inside Catherine. She asked no more about what I'd told her but seemed able to explore her own feelings now without worrying that she might be getting them wrong.

Part Two

THE THERAPY

6
CONTAINMENT

In some ways, counselling with young people is straightforward. A small child runs indoors crying, having fallen over and grazed its knee. Its mother scoops it up and sits the child down. 'Tell me *all* about it,' she says softly. Sobbing, the child recounts the story of what happened and what they were playing and how much it hurt and how it's still hurting. But not so badly now. In fact, it's feeling better. And, standing up, the child goes out to play again.

This is essentially what a counsellor is doing – listening, soothing and understanding until the hurt knee feels better. Very straightforward. But what's *not* straightforward is the way in which that listening, soothing and understanding is done when the grazed knee is a life story and crying masks a range of other, less accessible, feelings. It's not straightforward when the mother-counsellor has never met the child before but must immediately inspire confidence in their relationship. It's not straightforward when the child is instinctively wary or scared or resentful of mothers. And it's not straightforward when the child has never learned to talk about what hurt knees feel like.

Winnicott (1965) would describe the mother as 'holding' her child's distress: not running away from it, not immediately calling an ambulance and not bursting into tears herself. Instead, she stays calm. She bears her child's crying. She knows that there's nothing much she can do practically – perhaps wash the knee with water, perhaps put on a plaster – because the fact is that hurt knees *do* hurt and, usually, there's nothing to do but stay with her child until the hurt subsides. The child hasn't yet learned how to 'hold' or bear its own feelings – the hurt, the shock, the fear – so runs to its mother who calmly and patiently models for the child how to do it: how to wait until the pain passes, how to trust that it will pass, how to be distracted by thinking of other things.

Bion (1963) would be interested in the mother's capacity to 'contain' the distress: in her 'holding' or bearing of it, for sure, but also in her capacity to go on and help the child think about the experience, make sense of it, thinking about it *as an experience* of distress. Mawson (1994) explains:

> From infancy we evolve the expectation that we can gain some relief from these [disturbing states of mind] by seeking a 'container' for the painful feelings and the part of ourselves that experiences them. Partly, we unconsciously try to rid ourselves of them, but there is also the hope that the recipient of the projected distress might be able to bear what we cannot, and, by articulating thoughts that we have found unthinkable, contribute to developing in us a capacity to think and to hold on to anxiety ourselves. (p.70)

Containment is where counselling begins. Ruszczynski (2007) writes that 'Without the experience of containment, no development of a psychological self can take place, a self that can process and think about experiences and psychic states' (p.40). In some schools uncontained feelings are everywhere, with young people forever enacting feelings, unable to keep them to themselves, enacting them at their own and at other people's expense: cutting, swearing, blaming, bullying. And sometimes members of staff will be enacting their own feelings: dashing round, exuding stress, shouting and threatening, over-reacting to situations. Occasionally, too, there are uncontained counsellors: too busy to listen, hurrying ostentatiously from crisis to crisis, problem-vampires pumped up on the adrenalin of other people's distress.

In schools where these behaviours are commonplace, there's a sense of everything being out of control. The bell seems to ring especially loudly. Lessons are always being interrupted. Everyone's late. Nothing ever goes to plan and, as a result, everyone's anxious. It's impossible to relax and concentrate as the school lurches from one incident to the next.

I've written elsewhere (Luxmoore 2000) about youth workers containing the incipient anxieties of young people by never over-reacting, by behaving as if everything is going to plan and, as they move about, by always walking slowly. Most teachers quickly learn to do this in order to survive in the profession. They enter classrooms quietly. They smile calmly. They use eye-contact and other gestures to communicate disapproval, saving words for later and reserving the nuclear option of shouting only for some truly apocalyptic situation.

But the potential is always there for anxiety to be uncontained. Teachers have many practical things that they can do as they respond to situations, whereas counsellors have almost nothing. Somehow counsellors have to listen to the most distressing or bizarre stories in a way that's calm but robust. Somehow they have to find ways of connecting with young people without being swept away on tides of sadness and anger. They have to contain the anxieties of young people wanting answers, wanting the counsellor to make everything all right. They have to contain it when they feel like giving up themselves and they have to contain the anxieties of colleagues wanting to give up, wanting quick fixes, wanting the transformation of a student's behaviour...

'This school's a joke, the amount of work they expect teachers to do!'

'Go on,' says the counsellor.

'Well, all I ever seem to do is work!'

'That bad?'

'Absolutely that bad! No one listens! No one cares if you don't have a life out of school! They just expect more and more!'

'And they probably feel the same...'

'Maybe. But if they do, they don't show it! We do all this work and no one notices! No one ever says thank you!'

'It can be a lonely job…'

'Not just that! It can be a pointless job with all the paperwork we're expected to do. Most of which has got nothing to do with teaching!'

'Nothing to do with what you enjoy…'

'Nothing at all! Sorry, I shouldn't be sounding off like this. But, hey, it feels good to have a rant!'

From time to time, teachers do need to sound off. Otherwise, they'd end up enacting their frustrations at other people's expense. So I don't begrudge them the time I spend in corridors or car parks, listening as they complain. They deserve the time. A counsellor has a clinical supervisor with whom he or she can let off steam whereas teachers, whose jobs involve sustaining hundreds of human relationships every week, have nothing like that.

Hazel comes to see me, fuming because the headteacher has refused her permission to miss a day's work in order to attend her aunt's funeral.

On the face of it, there's nothing to say. The headteacher is quite within his rights and his decision is consistent with other decisions he's made when staff have wanted time off. But Hazel is a hard-working, conscientious teacher (as I'm sure the headteacher knows) and she's outraged.

'Who does he think he is? After all the hours I've put in for him, year after year? All the extras? All the evenings when I don't have to be here, but I am? And then I ask for *one day*! *One day* and it's refused! I could have called in sick like other people would have done but, no, I did it the proper way and look what happens! I'm an idiot, that's what I am! An absolute idiot! He talks about loyalty! How much loyalty is he showing me?'

And so she goes on. I know that the headteacher will have agonised about this. But that's irrelevant. She's upset. Almost certainly, there'll be a context. The death of her aunt may have got Hazel thinking about the prospect of her mother's death. Loyalty may also be a subject close to her heart. And it may be that she needs to feel special at the moment – hence her special request – and that need may be connected to all sorts of other things in her life.

As she continues, I ask myself what she needs from me right now? Has she come here to explore the meaning of this experience in relation to her life as a whole? Or has she come to rant, knowing that I won't probe her with questions, won't tell anyone about our conversation and won't think any the worse of her just because she's temporarily given in to an uncontained sense of injustice? I decide that it's the latter.

There's a lull. She needs me to say something.

'Shit, eh?'

'Yes,' she says. 'Shit, shit, shittety-shit!'

Ten minutes later, she finishes her tea and departs, calmer, promising to drive home safely.

Other members of staff will be regularly doing what I'm doing: letting their students and colleagues rant, knowing that the fit will pass. The headteacher will be doing this a lot, checking her watch to see how much time she can give to any particular person and deciding whether there's anything practical that she can do to help.

Young people and staff often come to the counsellor rather than to colleagues or to the headteacher when they sense that there's nothing to be done but are wanting to talk and think about what's happened. Initially, they ask for advice, ask what they should do. When the magician has no wand, they struggle to hide their disappointment. But then we go on to think about the meaning of whatever's happened: disappointment is still disappointment but the sense we make of it is forever changing. In fact, the end of counselling is realising that – actually – there's no cure; we may be able to improve our lives a little along the way but the important things in life won't change: our parents will always be imperfect, our most urgent wishes will usually be frustrated and death will still be waiting, however wonderful our achievements and however virtuous our lives. Counsellors help us to live with these truths; they help us to think about and contain our resulting rage and despair. Counselling in schools is ultimately about helping students and staff survive when things go wrong: when people are working hard but not succeeding; when they're deserving but not chosen; when they have no control over situations; when those who matter most are dying or dead. As Yalom (1980) writes: 'The ultimate task of therapy… is to help patients reconstrue that which they cannot alter' (p.273).

I listen and sympathise. 'It sounds really hard…'

'It is!'

The story continues. I ask about feelings that might have gone unnoticed – the hatred bubbling under the mask of respectability, the rage under the rationality, the fear under the years of experience, the relief under the grieving.

The person sitting opposite is surprised and glad to have been able to acknowledge some of these things. Before leaving, he looks up, as if to ask, 'I don't suppose that there's anything you can…?' and, meeting my gaze, looks away again, as if to say, 'No, I didn't think so!'

I've always wanted to call a book 'Shit Happens' because it's a phrase that young people use which encapsulates so much of what a counsellor's work is about: helping people to think about whatever's happened, helping them to bear and contain it, knowing that it's not as personal as it feels, that things *do* go wrong, that they're *not* fair but that sometimes there's nothing more to be done.

In my experience, schools able to contain the anxieties of students and staff tend to be creative places, and schools unable to do this aren't. Some schools try to convince themselves that all's well by creating illusions of containment: a slavish belief in the headteacher, for example, or a lengthening list of rules to cover every eventuality. Some schools create scapegoats whenever the going gets tough or set up some common enemy to hate and blame. The illusions eventually break down: the great leader turns out to be fallible; the anxieties multiply along with the rules; the scapegoats are crushed but must immediately be replaced; the common enemy refuses to fight back. Anxieties are passed up and down the line in the hope that someone will be able to contain them…

For example, a boy's mother argues with him at breakfast about the state of his bedroom. He leaves the house in a temper and picks an argument with the first teacher he encounters at school. Riled, that teacher takes her annoyance out on the deputy headteacher as she complains about the heating system in her classroom. The deputy headteacher is irked because heating problems aren't his responsibility but it seems as if everyone in school expects him to fix every problem. He bumps into the headteacher and vents his frustration, not about the heating of classrooms, but about the governors' decision to cut the maintenance budget and spend money instead on a new state-of-the-art reprographics department.

With some headteachers, the buck stops there. They're able to contain all the frustration, anger and disappointment coming their way. But some pass it on *unconsciously*, finding an excuse to telephone and berate a local education official about the way in which the school's special circumstances appear to have been overlooked – yet again – in the latest funding allocations. Some headteachers, also unable to contain the hostility coming their way, retaliate. The deputy headteacher is told that his point about the maintenance budget is noted and reminded that he's behind with his programme of lesson observations. An hour later, still angry at the unfairness of this, the deputy headteacher meets the teacher with the badly heated classroom. He pauses in the corridor to tell her that two of her highest-achieving students have complained that they're being held back by the behaviour of other students in her lessons. 'I'm sure it's nothing serious but just so that you know,' he says, smiling. She walks off, furious with him and with the two students concerned because she's already given them hours of extra time out of lessons. Later in the day, still fuming, she sees the boy with whom she had the argument at the start of the day. His tie is undone. When he protests, she threatens him with punishment. He wanders off, cursing under his breath, and, an hour later at home, swears at his mother, who responds by telling him to get out of the house and never come back.

Containing or uncontaining, schools take their unconscious lead from their headteachers, but a counsellor will be one of the people behind the scenes also helping to set the tone, containing some of the most acute anxieties, including anxieties about and caused by the headteacher. And containing the anxieties *of* the headteacher.

I've been lucky to work for headteachers who have been good at containing their own anxieties (*not* passing them on, *not* retaliating) but using me from time to time to talk things through, to rant or to be irreverent, cursing the unfairnesses of the job. In this respect, the counsellor's position in a school is unique: managed (ultimately) by the headteacher but not using the headteacher as others would use their manager for two reasons. Firstly, because the counsellor has a clinical supervisor with whom to discuss the dynamics of casework and, secondly, because the headteacher has never worked as a counsellor, so can't advise and direct a counsellor in the same way that he or she might advise and direct a fellow teacher. The counsellor is therefore slightly different: *consilieri* yet employee, peer yet underling. If the headteacher and counsellor respect each other and work well together, then the chances of a school containing its anxieties are good. If they don't, then the dangers are increased of everyone's anxieties spilling out and of the splitting I'll describe in the next chapter becoming a habitual way of dealing with difficulties.

7 AMBIVALENCE

Just as the curious, sceptical teachers in Chapter 3 might sit in the staffroom and ask the new counsellor 'What exactly is it that you do?', so a clinical supervisor might ask 'What exactly is it that you're trying to do with this person? What exactly is it that needs to happen therapeutically?' The supervisor is really asking for what Bramley (1996) calls a 'dynamic formulation'. In other words, 'What's the core, internal conflict here? What's got stuck developmentally? What's the underlying tension? You've listened and empathised... Now what's the therapeutic aim?'

It may well be that the counsellor doesn't yet know – after all, things sometimes emerge slowly – but unless the counsellor is going to spend weeks and months aimlessly following a young person down conversational blind alleys, he or she needs to be developing a working hypothesis, a sense of where the therapy needs to go in order to be guiding the young person gently in that direction.

Sometimes there are short-term ends. 'He needs to express his feelings,' says the counsellor, or, more specifically, 'He needs to express his anger'. But these short-term ends will be part of a bigger picture. Expressing feelings is where therapy starts, not where it finishes, and so, pushed, the counsellor elaborates, 'The problem is that he's learned to think away his feelings,' she says, or, 'He's learned to turn every feeling into some sort of anger.' Another way of putting these things is that he's learned to split.

Nine times out of ten, therapy with young people involves moving from Klein's (1946) paranoid-schizoid to depressive position or, less theoretically, involves the young person developing a greater ability to bear ambivalence, no longer splitting the world into thinking or feeling, good or bad, love or hate, us or them.

Ambivalence is hard to bear because it means acknowledging that life isn't as simple as we thought. It means that we have mixed feelings and mixed motives and that other people will feel similarly mixed. 'The achievement of this capacity for ambivalence, in reality a life-long struggle', writes Ruszczynski (2007), 'is one crucial indicator of the potential for relatively healthy and mature relationships' (p.24). It takes a lifetime to accept that our parents, for example, instead of being good parents or bad parents, might actually be a mixture and that we ourselves might be a similar mixture of good and bad, of strengths and weaknesses: right about some things, wrong about others. Splitting defends us against the anxieties of ambivalence. It simplifies life.

However, as an aside, it's worth remembering that splitting isn't always pathological or even problematic. As Ogden (1986) writes: '...it must be emphasised that splitting is not simply a defense; it's even more basically a mode of organising experience' (p.47). Sometimes we learn from experience that there are right ways and wrong ways, safe behaviours and dangerous ones. Splitting may make psychological sense but sometimes makes practical and moral sense as well; sometimes it describes an entirely appropriate marking of personal boundaries; sometimes there *are* good guys and bad guys.

That said, there's a connection between young people's tendency to split and the fact that they're engaged in the necessary developmental process of splitting away from their parents to become more independent. It's as if their developmental job is to split and yet they can't entirely split because they still need their parents in all sorts of ways. Somehow they have to negotiate a path between becoming separate and remaining merged: a path to be negotiated both at home and at school. And it's a difficult negotiation (Glasser 1979). It's much easier to say 'I hate you!' than to say 'I hate *and* love you!' It's much easier to say 'You're nothing to do with me!' than to say 'I'm apart from you and part of you!' Fonagy *et al.* (2004) write:

> Real separateness implies an ability to recognise both difference *and* similarity, and it is paradoxically the latter rather than the former that may be a true mark of autonomy. The challenge to identity in adolescence comes from accepting not difference, but similarity. (p.321)

Most young people come to counselling with a firmly established split which, in a way, has served them well until now. 'I'm a failure... You're the best... He's useless... She's brilliant... I hate my dad... I love my mum...' The split has seemed to simplify things when the complexities of life would otherwise have felt impossible to bear. The trouble is that now, months or years later, the split is too simplistic. The young person senses that it's an unsustainable world view. Something has to change but the young person is stuck, still reciting the old simplicities, still striking the old attitudes.

Immediately after a first session with a young person, it's useful to scribble down a family tree because the roots of the young person's splitting will be in family relationships. Sam, for example, splits the school into teachers who are good and teachers who are bad. And he splits his peers in the same way. He's in trouble because of rows with 'bad' teachers and fights with peers he 'hates'.

'That's just the way I am,' he insists. 'Always been like that. Always will be!'

Lots of young people begin counselling by presenting themselves in this way: as unchangeable, moulded by circumstances beyond their control and quite happy to stay like that. Except that they've come to counselling, which suggests that they know something's not right. 'Always been like that. Always will be!' is really just a way of holding on to something familiar in an unfamiliar counselling room, holding on to the apparent certainty of bad teachers, good teachers, bad enemies, good friends.

He lives with his father, step-mother and their two small children. Plus his younger sister and a half-brother from an earlier relationship of his father's.

I ask about his mother.

'No idea!' he says. 'D'you mean, where is she? No idea. Haven't seen her since she left and that was six years ago. I don't think about her. Karen's always been more of a mum to me. I call her Mum.'

I ask what happened six years ago.

'Don't know and don't care! She decided that she didn't want to live with us, so she left. Never seen her since. She might be living in Spain or somewhere like that. I'm not bothered. She can do what she likes. If she wanted to see us, she'd have done it by now.'

'What can you remember about her?'

'About when she left? Nothing really. She just said she was leaving and that was it. She went. To be honest, it didn't make any difference. It was always Dad who did everything in the house anyway. She didn't even know how to cook!'

This may be an exaggeration. I ask Sam what it felt like when his mother left.

'Didn't feel like anything! Like I said, it didn't make any difference.'

Again, I suspect that this may be an exaggeration, a simplification. Sam's 15 now so would have been about nine years old at the time. Nine years of growing up and living with his mother: he'll have felt plenty of things about her leaving and the experience will almost certainly not have been as simple as the story he's now telling. But it's his story and he's sticking to it: a really simple story, probably to disguise really complex feelings; a story at the heart of who he claims to be, a story about a bad mother and a good step-mother, a story about not knowing or caring. This has become the way he manages his feelings, the way he keeps them safe. And it may well have been necessary to do this when he was nine years old and trying his best not to make things worse. If there was no one to listen at the time, then it would have made life easier if there was nothing to tell.

The trouble is that this has involved splitting his view of the world into good and bad. Developmentally, this may be where he got stuck at the age of nine, so that now, as a 15-year-old, he's still trying to see the world in these terms and the world (at least the world of school) is effectively saying, 'It's never that simple, Sam. You can't go on like this!'

We could spend time talking about whether his teachers are good or bad. We could spend time talking about whether his peers are good or bad. But underneath all this is a family story and that's where our conversation needs to go. That's where Sam's splitting starts.

'What was she like?'

'My mum? Can't remember.'

'What did she look like? What did she like doing? What things can you remember doing with her?'

'She liked drinking, I know that! And sitting on the sofa all day watching crap television. And not caring what the rest of us were doing!'

'What *were* you doing?'

'I don't know – playing and stuff. Can't remember!'

'Playing with toys? Playing with her?'

'Like I say, I can't remember. Playing with the dog probably. Anyway, that's not important. Why are you asking?'

It's a fair question. I explain to him that we all have a life story and that who we become depends a lot on that life story.

'So?'

'So when important things have happened to us, they're bound to have an effect on us. They're bound to affect how we see the world. When you were nine, Sam, you had to deal with a really difficult thing. And you did deal with it. But those things stay with us and sometimes they get in the way. Sometimes they affect everything. They might make us suspicious of other people. Or they might make us hate other people. Or they might make us never want to trust other people again.'

'If you say so,' he says, unconvinced but prepared to humour me.

'What do you know about your mum when she was younger?'

'Not a lot!'

'How did she and your dad meet?'

'No idea.'

'They must have been young...'

'I think they were at school. She was 15 or something and he was in the year above...'

'And they fell in love?'

This is an important question. Young people tell dismissive, simplified stories about their divorced or separated parents: 'They don't speak any more... He hates her... She's always criticising him... He's not allowed near the house... She's burnt all the photographs...' The cruellest thing is when parents, angry and hurt, insist to their children that they never loved each other in the first place.

Sometimes they did love each other. However painful it may be for warring parents to remember, there may well have been a time – however fleeting – when they did love or did at least fancy each other. Their child was conceived and born into that. Not necessarily into hatred and bitterness and resentment. Once upon a time, two people were together and had fun. They laughed. They talked. They had holidays. They told each other things. They thought they were right for each other... Looking back to the time before the split, it's painful to remember these things, even when they're true. It's hard for parents to believe that they could ever have had those feelings for each other. 'What fools we were! I don't think we were ever *really* in love...'

But for many parents it did feel like love at the time, and that matters. All young people are building a sense of who they are and the autobiographical story they tell will determine the way they see themselves. The terrible fact is that when a young person's story begins 'When I was born, my parents were fighting and I wasn't wanted' or 'My parents never loved each other – I don't know why they had me', it feels like an emptiness at the heart of everything; as if all those sweet words of reassurance ('We may not have loved each other but we loved you!') are false, false, false. For many young people, the uncertainty never entirely goes away. 'Am I loveable? Have I ever been loveable?'

Of course, there are parents who *didn't* love each other; there are young people who were conceived in anger or rape or sheer indifference; there are young people whose earliest years were characterised by neglect and abuse. Acknowledging this is painful. Finding any good internal object, any reason to feel loveable becomes difficult. And yet the young person *has* survived. In the absence of adequate parenting, he or she has attached to other people instead or – more typically – to a part of herself or to a kind of behaviour, to a cynical part of herself or to a smiling kind of behaviour, to a false self or to a way of splitting the world… Anything to survive. And it's worked until now, keeping the young person safe.

Sam's story is of parents who never loved each other, of a mother who didn't care. And yet there was a time when his parents were together at school and, probably for several years after that, a time when they chose to stay together. The simplicity of 'They Never Loved Each Other' is under threat.

'Once upon a time they might have loved each other,' I suggest.

Sam shrugs.

'How old are they now?'

'I think my dad's 36.'

'So your mum's 35. Which means that she had you when she was 20, after she'd been with your dad for five years. They must have been pretty solid together.'

'My dad had Graeme, though,' says Sam, reminding me about his half-brother. 'But he didn't stay with Graeme's mum.'

The story gets more complicated. Sam's parents started going out at school. They stayed together for 14 years. In the early years, Sam's father had an affair with another woman that produced a son, Sam's elder half-brother Graeme. Through all this, Sam's mother stayed with his father.

I ask if I've understood this correctly.

Sam nods as if he'd barely understood it himself.

'She must have loved him a lot,' I suggest.

He says nothing. I imagine that, for Sam, this is a new story, a new way of looking at things. It's a radically different story from 'They Never Loved Each Other' and from 'My Mother The Uncaring Slob'. It asks questions about his father's faithfulness and about what life might have been like for his mother all those years ago. What would cause a woman to decide to leave her children when she'd already been through so much? 'She Didn't Care' no longer makes much sense. Sam has to start telling himself a more complex story and it's this story that we'll develop over the weeks ahead, using the bits of information he knows and imagining the rest, exploring the many possibilities arising from these snippets of information. Therapeutically, we're freeing Sam from his stuck, nine-year-old splitting of the world into good guys and bad guys. We're helping him develop a 15-year-old's ability to tolerate some degree of ambivalence towards other people. If his 'Bad Mother, Good Step-mother' story becomes a thing of the past, then it follows that his 'Bad Teacher, Good Teacher' and his 'Bad Enemy, Good Friend' stories will also need to become things of the past.

As with young people like Sam, counselling with members of staff involves helping them move from a defensive tendency to split towards a greater ability to tolerate ambivalence and complexity. Stokes (1994) writes that:

> This is one unconscious reason why we form and join organisations: to provide us, through splitting and projection, opportunities to locate difficult and hated aspects of ourselves in some 'other'. Internal personal conflicts can be projected on to the interpersonal or even inter-institutional stage. (p.124)

What this means is that one teacher might vehemently describe the headteacher as good and the deputy headteacher as bad in order to avoid the fact that the teacher himself is capable of both good and bad things. Another member of staff might insist that School A is caring and School B uncaring. Schools and the people in them easily become the recipients of our many projected splits.

Given this, how does a school contain these projections without splitting apart and fighting itself? I once taught in a potentially very good school but a school that never overcame its political splits. In the staffroom, the left-wingers sat on one side, the right-wingers on the other, with any more nuanced opinion towards the middle. Staff meetings were a public stating and re-stating of established positions. Nobody moved on because we couldn't get past our splitting: we couldn't think together. And amongst the parents, there was a similarly vociferous splitting between those who saw exam results as the aim of education and those more interested in their child's personal development; a splitting between those parents passionately in favour of streaming and those equally passionate about mixed-ability teaching.

In this particular school, the battles were ostensibly political. Officially, we argued over whose educational ideas were better and, certainly, there were important educational arguments to be had. But underneath all this, *unofficially*, I think our anxieties were also about whether we were good enough teachers, whether we were liked by the students, whether we were working hard enough. These were the things we were never able to think about, the things we never addressed. And underneath their political posturing, the parents were probably preoccupied in a similar way with anxieties about whether they were good enough parents, whether they were loved by their children and whether they were doing enough for their children.

In a school, the effects of splitting can be seen in the quality of relationships. Where there's splitting there'll be bullying, scape-goating, blaming, marginalising. Sam and his teachers will be capable of doing this and, in a sense, the school as an institution will also be capable of doing it – praising some local schools, undermining the reputation of others.

Caught between factions, it's easy for a headteacher to become the unwitting embodiment of all this. Some headteachers deal with splitting behaviour by enforcing a dictatorship. That way, everyone is silenced, *no one's* voice is heard. Other headteachers try to deal with splitting by being unfailingly democratic because, that way, *everyone's* voice is heard. Neither of these approaches attends to the anxieties causing the splitting in the first place. People like Sam and schools like the one I've described start splitting when there's anxiety, when they're feeling unconfident and unvalued, unable to bear mixed feelings and the imperfections of life.

Sometimes it helps to name the splitting, making conscious what's unconscious and, in so doing, giving people more understanding of themselves. A counsellor can be well placed to do this. In another school where I'd recently started work, I remember the staffroom being characterised by a series of splits. The men vastly outnumbered the women; the old outnumbered and disliked the young; the arts staff didn't speak to the science staff and so on. People were scared and resentful of each other. As a result, the students picked up the anxieties of the parent figures and behaved badly towards each other.

On a whole-staff away-day, I remember there being much unfocused grumbling in public about the headteacher, the government, the parents, the students. We were blaming everyone else rather than looking at the quality of our relationships with each other. I stood up and said so, naming some of the splits that seemed to be occurring in the staffroom and the unhappiness that seemed to be the result. I mentioned the fact that the staffroom was divided into tight little seating areas. Everyone had their own area, with no one daring to sit anywhere else. I said that the staffroom was a frightening place to go into and that, far from being the supportive staff team we liked to describe ourselves as being, we were actually very unsupportive towards one another.

There was silence. A few diversionary comments followed before the headteacher – no doubt feeling responsible – intervened with conciliatory words and, quickly, we broke for coffee. The point was made, however. Nothing changed overnight but, when we returned to school at the start of the next week, the chairs in the staffroom had been completely reorganised!

At another school, the conversations I was having with individual members of staff in counselling seemed to suggest that a split was emerging between the younger and older teachers, with the younger ones (the majority) starting to throw their weight around and the older ones feeling unwanted. I wrote and published the following piece in the staff magazine:

LATE BUSES

MR OLD TEACHER *and* MR YOUNG TEACHER *sit in a deserted staffroom. Behind are pictures of students with medical problems, Union notices and a miscellany of cheap, out-of-date adverts for local gardeners, taxi firms and estate agents propped up and dangling from drawing pins.*

MR OLD: Do you know if there are late buses running for students this week?

MR YOUNG (*looks up from his laptop*): Certainly hope so. I've just spent the weekend planning what they're going to be doing after school this term so I don't want to miss a week or we'll never get everything finished.

MR OLD: I wish I had your energy! I spent the weekend visiting my mother and trying to arrange a cleaner for her. Surprising how difficult it is to find a cleaner nowadays. I've put postcards in shop windows and so far had one phone call. One call! So now I've got to go all the way back up there next weekend to meet with a woman who might or might not turn out to be suitable.

MR YOUNG: Is your mother ill?

MR OLD: Not ill, exactly, but for the last few years she's had arthritis, which stops her getting around. And I'm the one who goes up to see her most weekends because my brother and sister live too far away. I feel bad about being so far away because she's on her own but you can only do what you can do. Parents can't help getting old. It's not their fault. I'd rather she kept her independence than went into a home. She'd hate that. Old age is just one of those things, isn't it, though no one seems to understand that at this school.

Checks MR YOUNG'S *response.*

They seem to want more and more for their money nowadays. I've always prided myself on working hard but if they're expecting me to work all through the night as well as all through the day then they know what they can do with their job!

MR YOUNG *embarrassed.*

They don't seem to realise that some of us have families. We can't spend all our lives working. No disrespect, but it's a lot easier when you don't have commitments.

MR YOUNG: I don't think I'll ever have kids. Teaching's hard enough without other responsibilities. All I ever seem to do is work!

MR OLD: Maybe. But you and the others still manage to go out together, don't you? You have your Friday nights in the pub and I know you meet up at weekends and go round to each other's houses. I'm always overhearing conversations about what went on.

MR YOUNG: That's true for some people. Some of us do enjoy a drink or two but you've got to have a bit of life, haven't you, after a hard week's work…

Pause.

Are you saying you wouldn't be a teacher if you had your time again?

MR OLD: I think about that. You get to my age and look back and wonder what it was all for. I remember when I was young it was the only thing that mattered. And I may be getting a bit cynical now but I still think it's the best job you can do – helping the next generation.

MR YOUNG: I agree. That's why I do it. Even if it does take up all my time.

MR OLD: So, no regrets so far?

MR YOUNG: To be honest, I'm not sure I'd do it again. Or at least I wouldn't do it until I was older. (*hesitantly*) Don't tell anyone at school but I've been thinking that I might do this year and then go travelling.

MR OLD: Good idea. Go and see the world. What does your girlfriend say about that?

MR YOUNG: I don't have a girlfriend.

MR OLD: Oh, I just assumed…

MR YOUNG: That's one of the reasons I'd like to go travelling. The thought of being a teacher and working flat-out for the rest of my life…

MR OLD: Do you live with other people?

MR YOUNG: I'm sharing a house with friends from university but one of them's moving out next summer to get married and another's applying for jobs in London. He works in computing so he's bound to get snapped up, lucky bugger!

MR OLD: So you'll be left on your own.

MR YOUNG: Exactly!

MR OLD: I see what you mean. Coming home to an empty house isn't much fun.

MR YOUNG: No, I don't mind that. The bit about the job that I do resent is not having any time to do anything apart from teach. I don't mind the pressure. It's just the feeling of life passing you by. And the feeling that you're expected to get on with it and no one notices as long as your results are good.

MR OLD (*unsympathetic*): At least you don't get people criticising you all the time. Us older teachers are made to feel as if nothing you do is ever good enough, that your experience counts for nothing. They're only interested in younger teachers – and that's partly because they're cheaper. If you notice, it's always the younger teachers who get the plaudits. And younger teachers are great – don't get me wrong. They're the ones the students seem to like. They're the popular ones. But when did one of the young teachers last go for promotion and not get it?

MR YOUNG: I don't know. It hasn't happened to me, if that's what you mean! I've got my work cut out just doing my job.

MR OLD: You get to my age and all you get is pressure. Pressure from work, pressure from home, pressure from your own kids… Our youngest has just gone off to university so now it's just me and Sally.

MR YOUNG: That must be nice…

MR OLD: Don't know about 'nice'. It does have its upside but you miss them when they're gone and it costs a fortune getting them through university. Then they come back and they're out seeing their friends all the time. To be honest, you feel a bit redundant. Mind you, it's not easy for young people nowadays, what with house prices and things like that.

MR YOUNG: I think I've accepted that I'll never own a house.

MR OLD: Couldn't your parents help you out?

MR YOUNG: They probably would if they could but I've never met my dad and my mum certainly couldn't help.

MR OLD (*embarrassed*): Oh, right.

MR YOUNG (*seeing* MR OLD's *embarrassment*): That's okay. I've always had to work for my own money. It's one of the things that makes me want to succeed in teaching – knowing how few jobs there are that are actually interesting and worthwhile.

MR OLD: You've never met your father?

MR YOUNG *shakes his head.*

MR OLD: Pity, you could have had mine, for what he was worth! All he did was hit us. That was all he knew. No idea how to be with us.

Both men silent, thoughtful.

MR OLD: I was the eldest so I got the brunt of it.

MR YOUNG: I'm the eldest as well! Weird that – we're both the eldest and both became teachers!

MR OLD: Must be all that taking responsibility. I wasn't always a teacher, though. Before teaching I was involved in music.

MR YOUNG *obviously surprised.*

MR OLD: Oh yes! My other life – you didn't know that, did you! I was a bass player. We were never signed or anything like that but we played up and down the country in all the best flea pits. Wine, women and song. Lots of that.

MR YOUNG: And sex?

MR OLD: Plenty of that around if you wanted it.

MR YOUNG (*intrigued*): A secret life! I never knew…

MR OLD: Well you wouldn't. We've never really spoken before today, have we!

MR YOUNG: I think it's a pity that people in the staffroom don't talk more. Do the students know that you were in a band?

MR OLD: I've told one or two of them over the years but they're not interested and I can't bear the stuff they listen to nowadays. So I'm afraid we pass each other by. I've got my life and they've got theirs.

MR YOUNG: You should come for a drink on a Friday.

MR OLD: I'd be completely out of place. I wouldn't know what you were talking about half the time. I appreciate the offer but, to be perfectly honest, I don't think us oldies would be particularly welcome, even if we did show up.

MR YOUNG: Or come to one of the gym sessions? Lots of people go, including some of the admin staff. You don't have to be particularly fit and we usually go for a swim in the pool afterwards.

MR OLD (*deliberating*): Don't take this the wrong way because I don't find you to be like this… But the thing that puts me off is some of the younger members of staff seeming to think they know it all. Sometimes it feels like they're looking at you as if they can't wait for you to retire. It pisses me off, if you'll pardon my French. And then I think, well sod you, bunch of know-alls! When you're a bit older, you'll realise!

MR YOUNG: That's fair enough, but I know there are some people who feel patronised by older staff as well. There are some older members of staff who act like they own the school because they've been here so long. And all they ever do is talk about the good old days. They never even bother to say hello.

MR OLD: You mean people like me?

MR YOUNG: No, not you. But there are some people who can make you feel really small. And they do it in front of students. I don't know why they feel they've got to do it! Everyone already respects them. They already know how to teach – the rest of us are still learning.

MR OLD: Maybe, but you've got to remember that you're lucky. You've got your future ahead of you. Some of us have got nothing to look forward to – not really – except retirement, old age, illness and then the big sleep.

MR YOUNG: Is that what you think? About dying?

MR OLD: Sometimes. But mostly I just get on with it.

MR YOUNG: I think about dying. I think about getting older and what the point of my life will have been.

MR OLD: Really?

MR YOUNG: Of course!

MR OLD: Now you're making me miserable!

MR YOUNG: Why?

MR OLD: Only joking! It's fair enough, what you're saying.

MR YOUNG: I was only saying what you were saying.

A bell rings loudly. MR OLD *and* MR YOUNG *look at each other, uncertain. They get up reluctantly, gather their things and EXIT.*

The potential for splitting between older and younger members of staff is always there. Working with younger colleagues, older staff are likely to be reminded of their own (lost) youth and own (unfulfilled) potential. And for their part, younger staff will always have strong feelings about older colleagues – the parent figures who've been running things for so many years and only partially succeeding.

Counsellors may be well aware of the dangers of splitting in the staffroom. But school counselling services are perfectly capable of splitting themselves off from the rest of the school in order to manage their own anxieties about being good enough or valued enough. Sometimes this splitting is provoked by geography: the service has been put or has deliberately put itself in rooms away from the rest of the school. Sometimes it's provoked by the service coming to see itself as representing feelings while the rest of the school represents thoughts. Sometimes it happens because the service has come to represent 'soft female' rather than 'hard male' qualities.

Believing that counselling can save the world is just another kind of splitting. It goes without saying that, until a counselling service integrates itself into the life of the school, acknowledging the counsellor's own ambivalent feelings ('I love this school and I hate this school; I feel valued and unvalued'), it can have little influence over the splitting tendencies of anxious young people and staff.

8
THE OUTSIDE AND
THE INSIDE

Maria doesn't arrive for our first meeting so I'm obliged to go and fetch her. She's sitting at the back of her lesson, away from the other students, presumably separated so that she can't spoil their concentration by doing whatever it is that Maria does. She sees me, mouths 'Oh fuck! Sorry!', gathers up her things and follows me out of the classroom, ignored by her peers.

Because she's on the verge of being permanently excluded from school, her teachers have put in place all sorts of rules and imaginative kinds of support for her. Nothing works. They try again. Still nothing works, and her life away from school is becoming ever more chaotic in the meantime.

We walk to the counselling room. Already we know each other a little from corridor conversations and I've worked with two of her friends in the past. She might have agreed to meet with me because they've reported favourably. She might be coming because she fancies doing something other than sitting at the back of a classroom, pretending to work when she can't understand, having missed too many lessons. She may have struck a deal with her teachers and is coming to see me as part of that deal, although she'll know from her friends that counselling isn't necessarily an easy option. My guess is that she's coming because she's prepared to give one more professional a go, even at this late stage… 'See if this one's any good. See if this one understands. See if this one knows how to change my shitty life!'

She starts with grandiose tales about friends who have died ('You wouldn't know them!'), fights she's been in ('I can't help it!'), times when she's been arrested ('The police all know my name!') and times when she's passed out drunk ('What a laugh!'). She mentions a father who's disowned her and a mother who hates her ('They've given up!').

This is normal stuff: I'm interested but not impressed. I don't doubt that many of these things will have happened but, for Maria, this is the shield she erects as if – sitting down in my room – she pulls big, grandiose cushions around her for comfort and protection. The challenge is to relax the shield a little without breaking it down because, like all defences, it's doing an important job, keeping Maria safe. We have to find a way of talking about what's behind it, what it protects, and we have to do this in a way that doesn't shame or scare her. Winnicott (1971) writes of 'the individual engaged in the perpetual human task of keeping inner and outer reality separate yet interrelated' (p.2). If her outside shield can be more accepting of her inside fears and hurts and longings, then Maria might feel better able to accept the world with its mistakes, its mixed motives, its many faults and imperfections.

'Presumably, the people who don't know you only see these things,' I say. 'Presumably, they just think you're a fighter, a drinker, a laugh, and don't realise that you're also someone who's serious about her life, who cares a lot and gets angry and hurt when things aren't fair…'

She hasn't exactly told me these things so I'm putting words into her mouth, inviting her to disagree. But if I've timed it right, she won't say no and – implicitly – we'll have named some of the things on the *inside*: her seriousness, her caring, her anger, her hurt, her sense of justice and injustice.

She looks taken aback. 'Yeah, I suppose…'

For young people, one of the difficulties of allowing anyone to know what's inside is the unfairness of it: 'Why should I? Why should I tell people things about myself when they don't tell me things about themselves?' Maria will have sat in school offices with parents and teachers expecting her to tell them what's inside. 'Why do you do it, Maria? Why do you behave like this?' She might have known the answers – why she refused to surrender her phone, why she swore, why she stormed out, why she slammed the door so hard that the glass broke – she just won't have been prepared to tell these people when they've told her nothing of what *they* feel inside: her mother trying to look stern while secretly angry with her father; her father trying to look relaxed while secretly hurt because Maria isn't speaking to him at the moment; Mr Pimm, the deputy headteacher, trying his best to look commanding while secretly afraid that Maria will swear at him. And Mrs Thomas, the teacher who deals with her on a daily basis, looking kind and concerned while secretly furious with Maria for taking up so much of her time... Adults also have an outside and an inside and it frustrates young people when adults share nothing of this. 'Why should I tell you anything?' Maria might ask. 'Why should I? You expect me to talk about stuff but you never do!'

With five minutes of our session left, she reaches into her bag and brings out her make-up. Ignoring me, she holds up a small mirror and re-applies mascara, foundation, lipstick. She brushes and adjusts her hair, curling it this way and that, trying for the best effect.

I say that she's skilled with her make-up.

She doesn't reply.

'It's important for you to look good, Maria.'

She agrees. But it's as if she's withdrawing, preparing herself for the challenge of break time, putting her outside back on in order to look as attractive and confident as possible before heading off to the canteen to rendezvous with friends.

So where does this leave me as her counsellor? How much do I maintain an outside and an inside myself? How much do counsellors generally – often trained to reveal as little as possible about themselves – share with young people what they're actually thinking and feeling inside?

A school counsellor is in a wonderful position to model a bearing of this tension between the outside and the inside. The counsellor will be an insider like everyone else in the school and yet an outsider in that the role of counsellor is different. In the school where I work, I'm a member of staff with an identity badge like every other member of staff but, instead of being 'Sir' or 'Mr Luxmoore', I'm 'Nick' – different from other members of staff. The way the counsellor manages confidentiality also says something about the bearing of this tension: keeping things absolutely confidential but in a relaxed way, not barking at people who want to know more than they can be told. The outside and the inside must find ways of co-existing. As I described in the last chapter, what goes on inside the counselling room can't be cut off from what goes on outside it. I'll fetch Maria from her lesson. As we walk back to the counselling room together, we'll talk. We'll continue to talk inside the room.

The next time we meet, I mention that I've cycled to our appointment because I'm banned from driving.

'What? You're actually banned?'

I tell her that I've been speeding and hate not being able to drive my car.

'Well,' she says sternly, 'it's your own fault!'

In telling her this, I'm not telling her more than she needs to know. I'm not baring my soul or asking her to become my counsellor. In a minute we'll get back to talking about her week. All I'm doing is sharing with her something that she hadn't expected and didn't know; sharing a little of what's inside me at the moment, a frustration, a small vulnerability.

We talk about her latest row with her parents. They were angry because she came home late on a school night. When I suggest that they may not understand why staying out and seeing her friends in the evening matters so much to her, Maria confirms that, yes, most people don't know what she really feels. 'They think they do but they don't. They know my name but not my story!'

'I suppose it's hard for them to know,' I say, 'because we're not always good at letting people know things. We get hurt – all of us – and learn to hide what we're feeling so that we won't get hurt again.'

She's listening, interested.

'We all have a shield that protects us. Sometimes we go round with our shield, pretending not to care. Sometimes the shield helps us to go quiet and not say anything. Sometimes it helps us to act angry and tell people to piss off. But we all need our shields. Yours is very good at protecting you, Maria. No one would ever know what you were really feeling!'

Affirming the importance of a young person's defences is important. As I said in Chapter 5, counselling is never about trying to strip away defences but about trying to *understand* them – how they developed, why they developed, the dangers they were designed to avert. When Maria, in all her stroppiness, feels that her outside and her inside have been properly understood, then she might feel able to hold on to her shield less tightly, less habitually; she might feel more confident about developing new, more relaxed, more generous responses to life's frustrations.

And she's more likely to loosen the hold she has on her shield if she experiences other people loosening theirs. In schools it can be difficult to find these people. Most schools have an outside 'image' which is often quite at variance with what goes on in the corridors and classrooms. Young people are well aware of this and are scornful of the public relations stunts, the classrooms tidied up for visiting dignitaries, the entreaties to behave well and make a good impression when the inspectors arrive. They call it 'bullshitting' and 'being two-faced'. They hate it.

There's a connection between a school's use of a shield and a young person's use of a shield. Like any parent figure, the school will model a way of dealing with life when things are difficult, either pretending that it's not happening and isn't affecting everyone or acknowledging that it *is* happening and *is* affecting everyone. When the outside pretence and the inside reality of a school are dramatically at odds with each other, young people take their cue, keeping their own outside and inside determinedly separate. Whatever a school can do to bridge the divide helps everyone, therefore. Instead of pretending that everything's wonderful, some schools encourage parents to visit during a typical school day to 'see us as we really are'. This helps. Some schools consult with students about all aspects of school life, ensuring that the public relations hype never gets ahead of the daily reality. This helps. I remember working with one headteacher who was particularly good at demystifying himself, making it clear that, while remaining our boss, he was a fallible human being like the rest of us. Because of his honesty, students and staff respected him more rather than less.

I've worked fairly closely with Mrs Thomas for the last two years, ever since she got the job of managing students like Maria. At the time, I congratulated her and she seemed pleased, saying that she'd need all the help she could get. Since then, we've discussed students we've had in common and I've made a point of passing on their comments whenever they've told me good things about her.

'You can tell Mrs Thomas cares because she actually listens, even if she does get arsy sometimes!'

'Can I tell her that?'

'If you want. Don't tell her the arsy bit, though!'

So my relationship with Merlene Thomas has always been good, and now, as our latest conversation about Maria finishes, she adds, 'Can I pop in sometime?'

'D'you mean, make an appointment?'

'If that's all right,' she says, 'It's not urgent. I know how busy you are. Just any time you're free. I've been thinking it might be useful to talk over a few things.'

Ten days later, I'm making her a cup of tea in my counselling room and she's enthusing about the fact that – so far this week – Maria hasn't got into trouble.

She thanks me for the tea. 'I need this!'

I say nothing.

She looks thoughtful and her eyes fill with tears. She reaches for a tissue, unable to speak. 'Sorry!' she gulps. 'I knew this would happen!' The tears won't stop despite her frantic dabbing. 'I'm sorry, Nick! You can see why I've been putting off coming to see you. I'm sorry. You must get sick of people crying all the time!'

I say something about it being an honour to be trusted.

'I just don't know how much longer I can keep this up...'

'Meaning work? Or other things?'

'Work,' she says. 'Well, I say "work" but there are probably other things. I don't know.'

Again, I say nothing.

'Work is all I do. And that's the problem. When I'm not at work, I'm thinking about work. I'm not sleeping properly. I don't do anything useful at home. My husband's very patient but you can tell he's getting fed up with me. I've even wondered about going to the doctor in case I'm depressed… What do you think?'

I say it would be good to hear more.

'I like my job,' she says. 'Don't get me wrong. I wouldn't swap it for anything. And I like the kids, even if they can be little buggers sometimes… I'm sorry,' she says, continuing to dab her eyes. 'I really don't know what's the matter with me today!'

'This might sound like a funny question,' I say to her, 'but why do you do the job, Merlene? I know we all have bills to pay and sometimes mouths to feed, but there are easier ways of earning a living than working with difficult young people day in and day out. Why do you do it, really?'

She says she doesn't know. 'I sort of fell into it. I've always been someone who likes to help. I was a nurse before I had children. But this job – I don't know – it sort of gets hold of you. There's so much pressure all the time and it just goes on and on. You think you've solved something, or at least made it better, but then another five things come along that need sorting out by yesterday, to add to the list of fifty things already waiting!'

I ask about her original family – what her father would say about all this, what her mother would say – casting around for voices from the past driving Merlene on to feats of unending self-sacrifice. In effect, I'm looking for critical superegos in the expectation that we might then spend some time beginning to answer them back, putting them in their place. But I can't find them. Apparently her father was happy with whatever his daughter did and her mother was easy-going. Merlene's own children sound settled in their various occupations. She worries about them, of course, but doesn't seem to be projecting any of those worries onto the school students for whom she's now responsible. In other words, she's not supporting

Maria in order to resolve something about her relationship with her own children. I ask about her husband, wondering whether their relationship has some bearing on her work... Is she working so hard in order to escape from him? Is she proving something to him? Is she using work to fill some gap in their relationship? But no. She sounds fond of him: exasperated with him at times but loyal and appreciative.

'I can't go on like this,' she says, returning to the start of our conversation, her tea finished and her tears long gone. 'I feel like I'm trapped. Something's got to change.'

I ask what it would be like to give it all up.

'I couldn't do that!'

'Why not?'

'I just couldn't.'

'You could,' I say. 'Any of us could give up our jobs. We wouldn't have any money coming in but we could give up our jobs!'

She looks unconvinced. 'I *feel* like giving up sometimes,' she concedes. 'In fact, I feel like giving up a lot!'

'Really?'

'Every night! I lie there thinking about not having to go to work tomorrow and not having twenty new messages every time I open my inbox. I think about staying at home. Going to the shops. Seeing friends and not feeling tired all the time. Cooking decent meals. Even trying a new recipe!'

'Maybe you've become your job,' I suggest. 'Maybe we lose track of ourselves sometimes and the job takes over? Maybe you've lost track of yourself?'

'How do you mean?'

'Well, maybe in order to do the job so effectively you've had to forget about parts of you that are important. I imagine that in this job you have to be calm all the time and fierce sometimes and always patient and never complaining...? Maybe you never get to have a rant? Or tell people what you really think? Or swear at a few parents? Or have time for students who *aren't* in trouble? Or put your feet up in the staffroom and tell rude jokes?'

She laughs. 'You've hit the nail on the head there! I don't even know any rude jokes these days! But how am I supposed to change anything? I don't know how to change anything.'

I say that I don't know either, 'But we could keep meeting and we could tell some rude jokes! We could use the time together to tell it like it is, the way you really feel it, Merlene. Not the way you pretend. If you're pissed off with school, we could talk about it here because you certainly won't be able to talk about it out there. Out there you have to be Mrs Thomas who's always calm and patient and in control of everything. In here, we can talk about things any way we want!'

'Sounds nice!'

'Shall we try it?'

'If it wouldn't take up too much of your time?'

We book another meeting in a fortnight and she goes off, joking about needing to practise her swearing. It could well be that our work will eventually be about *deserving* ('If it wouldn't take up too much of your time?') because, if Merlene has become institutionalised (Hinshelwood 2001), internalising the belief that she doesn't deserve anyone's time or care or love, the belief that she must dedicate herself to others without allowing herself to receive anything in return, then our meetings can begin to temper that belief. As with Maria, I think that the focus of our work will be on re-connecting Merlene's outside and inside: the professional and the personal. How can she continue to be a calm, containing presence with students like Maria while acknowledging her own dissatisfactions and rage, her frustrations and aloneness? How can she bear all the projections onto her without identifying with them, without starting to feel all that despair and anger herself? How can she be a dedicated professional while allowing herself a personal life full of friends and recipes and shopping and swearing? Her first step towards this has been daring to ask, 'Can I pop in sometime?'

9 A SENSE OF WORTH

Figures emerge from the darkness, singing quietly. Slowly the lights come up and a group of peasants is revealed, trying their best to look hungry and frightened while, at the same time, singing and moving stealthily across the stage. Clearly, something momentous is about to happen. I watch, willing them on, hugely impressed by the ambition of the show.

And then I see Katie. She's towards the back of the stage, behind the more confident peasants. Despite the make-up, it's definitely her. I check my programme and I'm right. She's less confident but perhaps that's appropriate for a hungry, frightened peasant, expecting to be shot at any moment, concentrating for all she's worth, unlike some of the peasants who are sneaking glances at the audience.

Katie Buckland! I had no idea that she was in the show and I'm delighted. I think back to our meetings: a shy girl telling me about being picked on and having no friends; a girl with divorced parents and a violent step-brother; a girl sitting passively while I tried my best to hear her feelings and re-connect her with any vivacity she may once have had.

I remember thinking that I'd failed. After a few sessions she decided not to continue, claiming to feel more confident now. I doubted that. She said she'd come back if she needed to, but I was sure that I'd never see her again and remember spending time in supervision wondering what I could have done differently, what I'd missed, what I'd misunderstood.

I wondered if I'd been too gentle. 'But I didn't want to scare her off,' I protested to my supervisor. 'I imagined that everyone else in her life would be brow-beating her and that we'd need to work on how she came to lose her confidence in the first place.'

'Why did she come to see you?' my supervisor asked.

I said it was the teachers' idea. 'I think they just thought she was unhappy.'

'Is that what Katie said?'

'No, I'm not sure that she said anything about why she'd come. I just assumed that she knew why she was there.'

I could see my supervisor thinking.

'Maybe she was always more robust than you gave her credit for? Maybe stopping counselling was her way of telling you that?'

This made sense. I hadn't been what Katie was looking for and needed to swallow my professional pride.

Most people come to counselling with poor or damaged self-confidence but counselling is only one of the *many* ways through which they develop self-confidence. Just as importantly, they might make a new friend, survive a Maths test, do well in their English coursework, get fit, excel on a work experience placement, spend time with a lovely teacher on a school trip. They might get involved in the school production. Six months ago, Katie dared to go to an audition because someone – and it wasn't me – probably sensed that she was perhaps secretly keen to be in the show. Someone encouraged her. It might have been a friend. It might have been a teacher. It might have been one of the cleaners or receptionists or maintenance workers. I'm reminded that I work in schools because I think it's possible to develop cultures supportive of everybody where a daily drip-feed of informal recognition and encouragement is as therapeutic as any formal counselling session. Counselling will play its part but counselling will only happen once a week or once a fortnight. What happens in school the rest of the time will be at least as therapeutic (or anti-therapeutic).

Our counselling sessions may have been underwhelming but I did one good thing with Katie. Whenever she didn't turn up, I went and fetched her from her lesson as I do with all students who don't turn up, most of whom have simply forgotten the time of their appointment. Their forgetfulness wastes time but, for many, being fetched is never a waste of time. Rather, it demonstrates to the young person that the counsellor *is* bothered, *isn't* deterred and *does* care enough to come after them. I suspect that, of the students who 'forget' their counselling appointments, some do so in order to see whether the counsellor will make this effort, fighting to continue the relationship even when the young person has made it difficult.

Our need for recognition is primitive (Luxmoore 2008). As babies, we develop a sense of self under the recognising, mirroring gaze of a parent. That parent or parent figure reflects us back to ourselves as worthwhile or insignificant, as interesting or dull, multi-faceted or narrow. Counselling is all about recognising people: recognising the interesting parts others don't see, the unspoken feelings, the unexpressed desires and fears. Recognition allows people to feel that they exist. Supportive recognition allows them to feel that they're worth something.

One of the simplest things a school counsellor can do is to learn names. Not just the names of the people using the counselling service – that's easy – but the names of everyone in school, staff and students alike: people who will never use the counselling service but who will be contributing all the time to a prevailing atmosphere. When people feel recognised, when they feel that they exist and are worth something, then they're more likely to find it in themselves to recognise other people as also worth something.

Counsellors will do this without getting much recognition themselves. As I described earlier in the book, they must live with a perpetual inability to rescue people from misfortune and make everything all right. Their own sense of worth must therefore be robust enough not to need the constant recognition of other people. The problem-vampires are those counsellors needing the constant recognition that comes with being The Only Person Who

Understands, The Only Person Who Can Help. 'Where would we be without our problem-vampire? We're all completely dependent on her!'

In moments of self-pity, counsellors might be tempted to think that they have a hard time, busily supporting everyone else while being self-effacing themselves, working with yet another troubled young person and never knowing exactly how the story will end. But it's worth remembering what it's like for teachers who, if they're honest, will admit that their best lesson, the one they spent half the night preparing, will still only engage 95 percent of the class. And that's their *best* lesson! At best, there will still be 5 percent of students not listening, not understanding, not making the connections. The percentage of students engaged by a standard lesson will be much lower. Yet these are lessons taught by conscientious, hard-working, experienced teachers. They know that they can't reach all the people all the time, however hard they try, however much they care, and they have to live with that. They know that there'll always be people on the sidelines – parents, school governors, politicians – pointing critical fingers, demanding more, demanding better, demanding perfection.

I suspect that most teachers work so busily in order not to think about these things. They develop ways of describing themselves which don't rely on the recognition of outsiders. 'We're a very supportive staff,' they say, or 'Of course, at this school we work with some of the most disadvantaged students,' or 'Compared to other schools, we lose out financially.' But these mantras are brittle. The need for recognition never goes away.

———

Carol contacts me, wondering if we can meet. She's about 50. I know her as someone who seems very competent, getting on with her job quietly and without fuss, rarely saying anything in staff meetings. Students speak well of her.

She's very late, leaving us only 20 minutes to talk. Oddly, she doesn't apologise. She hasn't been sleeping well, she says. The job seems to be getting harder with her young Head of Department – Dave – forcing the pace. She says she's started worrying about little things that she never used to worry about before. In fact, she's even thought of giving up teaching, 'But not seriously!'

'Why "not seriously"?'

'Well, I need the money for a start,' she says, smiling. 'I'm a single mother and, although my girls are older now, money doesn't grow on trees! Also, I *like* teaching. Or I used to like it before it got ridiculous.'

'Ridiculous with so much work?'

'There's no time,' she says. 'It's not so much fun any more. Everyone's running around, wanting this, wanting that. No one stops to think.'

'Or listen?'

'Ah well, they *never* listen!' she laughs. 'I've given up expecting that! That really *would* be asking a lot!'

'If they did listen, what would you tell them, Carol?'

She's surprised. 'I don't know. Probably what I've just told you!'

My question seems to have made her uncomfortable, defensive. I wonder whether I'm in danger of forcing the pace (like Dave) because we've got so little time to talk. I ask who's around at home and she tells me that she lives with her younger daughter who's in her last year at another school. Her elder daughter, a solicitor, lives in London with her barrister boyfriend. Carol and the girls' father divorced almost exactly ten years ago.

She changes the subject, as if all this is unimportant – silly psycho stuff. 'You know,' she says, 'I think I probably just need to do one of those Time Management courses.'

I feel as if I'm being slapped down by this competent teacher who never says anything in staff meetings: slapped down by quiet, unfussy Carol who's probably much angrier than she ever lets on and probably much sadder than she's prepared to admit. The trouble is that, by coming late to our meeting, she's sabotaged our chance to talk. I want to point this out, but don't.

I do decide to be firm. 'It's up to you, Carol, but I suggest that we meet again. Then we can have more time to discuss things.'

'Well, if you think it'll help,' she says. 'I was wondering if I should just go to the doctor and ask for sleeping pills.'

'I don't know if the two of us meeting will help,' I say. 'I can't promise anything. I do know, though, that a doctor will be interested in your sleeping but *more* interested in what's keeping you awake in the first place. My guess is that we get to stages in our lives when things don't make quite as much sense as they used to and we wonder what exactly we're doing. And when that happens, I think it's useful to talk with someone.'

I think she knows what I mean but – understandably – is probably in two minds about exploring a subject that might be difficult. So she wants to talk and doesn't want to talk, makes an appointment and sabotages it.

When we do meet again, she's only slightly late, with a story about how lucky young teachers are, having no commitments or dependants. I ask whether she was once one of those lucky young teachers.

'A long time ago,' she says ruefully. 'But I don't regret having children or anything like that. Not for one minute. In a funny kind of way, I don't even regret my marriage, even if it did turn out badly. We're still friends. No, I just envy the younger ones, that's all.'

'Including your daughters?'

'No, of course not! I love my daughters!'

'Your youngest will be leaving home soon…'

She hesitates, puzzled. 'Oh, I see where you're going! Yes, you're right. That does weigh on my mind.'

I say I'm not surprised. 'It's tough when we love people and have to let them go.'

She's about to speak but can't. Her eyes fill with tears. 'Sorry!' she says as the tears slide down her cheeks.

'It's sad, Carol.'

'It is! It is! But I'm happy really!'

'Of course you are. Though you'd be forgiven for feeling sad sometimes!'

Still wiping away tears, she says, 'I think that's it, really. I *am* sad!' She looks at me, checking, deciding. 'And it does get lonely when you're on your own, always on your bloody own! Do you know what I mean?' She blows her nose. 'Most of the time I'm fine but sometimes – and it's mostly when I can't get to sleep – I start thinking about what it's going to be like and that's…quite scary!'

'You mean, thinking about the future?'

'I suppose so. I'm a positive person, really. Always have been. But just recently, these last months, I don't know, I've started thinking…' She pauses. 'Do you know what I mean? I think that's the thing that's getting to me about teaching at the moment. Here I am, working hard, teaching everybody else's children, earning money for my girls who pretty soon won't be needing it… *Why?* Why am I bothering? What's in it for me?' She pauses again. 'I know we're supposed to do things for love and not for ourselves but, honestly, there are times when I wonder!'

'Wonder what you're worth?'

'Exactly! What I'm doing with my life! I know this sounds silly, but why aren't I having affairs? Or going round the world? Or seeing my friends? Or having time to read a book?'

I tell her that these are good questions.

'You think so? You don't think I'm mad, then? Or becoming a heartless little bitch who doesn't care about other people?'

I say I think she's a hard-working woman who cares about lots of people. Hundreds of people.

She smiles. 'Good!'

'But I still think they're good questions, Carol, and I do think it's hard to know what we're worth, especially as we get older. It's hard to know how we're supposed to be living our lives.'

'I'm so glad you've said that,' she says, 'because that's what I think about all the time. My mum died last year – my dad died years ago – but somehow when she was alive I felt as if I knew what I was supposed to be doing. And now that she's not around, it feels different…'

We'll go on to talk about her mother and about what the loss of her mother has been like. (I've also made a mental note to find out where the phrase 'heartless little bitch' comes from in Carol's life.) What we're really doing is *recognising* her: recognising despairing Carol, sad Carol, angry Carol, frightened Carol, sexual Carol ('Why aren't I having affairs?'). We're recognising that she isn't just another teacher behind with her paperwork and never saying anything in staff meetings; she isn't just another cog in the machine. The chances are that she'll sleep better for knowing that her anxieties and doubts are recognisable to another person.

Schools are good at recognising tangible achievements but don't really cater for doubts. Their rhetoric is all about realising everyone's potential 'before it's too late'. They focus on the future as an end in itself, never on what comes after that future. So when there are doubts about the meaning of the future (and the meaning of teaching and the meaning of middle-aged life), a person like Carol can end up feeling as if she's the odd one out, surrounded by younger colleagues who seem so certain, their heads buried in their careers, proving their worth with exam results, with promotions and, before long, with children of their own…busy, busy, busy. Once you raise your head and look around, like Carol, you start wondering what it's all for and whether anybody else is wondering the same thing. Working conscientiously with young people means believing that human beings are worth something and that good things might be in store for them. 'But what about me?' Carol might ask. 'What am I worth? What about *my* potential now that my children no longer need me, now that I'm single, now that my parents are dead and now that I'm no longer one of those young teachers with lots to say in staff meetings?'

Counselling provides a rare opportunity for these questions to be taken seriously and thought about in schools. For staff as well as for young people, they're questions which have a tangible bearing on a person's behaviour: unless her sleeping improves, Carol will find herself off work with a doctor's note. I've worked with hundreds of young people whose behaviour is also an expression of anxieties and doubts no one will address. They're the same anxieties, the same doubts that stop Carol sleeping at night: 'What am I worth? Who cares about me? What's all this *for*?' In counselling, they can be recognised as good questions worth thinking about; as interesting, important questions; not questions born of self-pity or stupidity. The sense of worth or 'self-esteem' that we promote in schools starts with a sense of self, and a sense of self starts with an experience of being recognised (Luxmoore 2008).

I ask Carol about her mother.

'She was lovely,' she says. 'Just an ordinary, loving mum. Always had time for us. Always listened. Always interested. Didn't judge. Thought that all her children were wonderful.'

She tells me stories, happy stories about her mother and describes the shock of finding out that her mother had cancer.

'She died two months later… How unfair is that? When you think of all the people who live long lives and then Mum goes and dies so quickly. And even when she was dying, she still wanted to know how everyone was doing. She was still asking how I was, what the girls were doing…'

'Not like people at school?'

'No,' she sighs, 'not at all like people at school!'

I ask what her mother would say, hearing how fed up she's feeling with school, with life, with everything.

'She'd say that you can only do what you can do. She'd say you've got to get on with your life. She'd say have fun, girl. Enjoy it. Leave teaching if you want but don't spend the rest of your life regretting things.'

'Good advice?'

'Good advice!'

'And what would she say about you, Carol? About you wondering whether anybody cares?'

Her eyes fill with tears again. But happy, sad tears.

10
THE ANXIETIES OF
NOT KNOWING

Kenny doesn't know. He doesn't know why his parents split up; he doesn't know if his mother's planning to have another baby; he doesn't know if he really fancies Charlotte and he doesn't know if his grandmother's cancer means that she's dying. Apparently unconcerned by any of these things, he slopes around, head down, saying little, irritating a succession of well-meaning members of staff who try to infuse him with their own energy and enthusiasm before concluding that 'Kenny's just so negative about everything!'

He has a reputation for never knowing where he's supposed to be or what he's supposed to be doing, but I wonder how much – for Kenny – not knowing is the story of his life. When everyone else seems so purposeful, confident and clear about their lives, I wonder whether not knowing about his own life makes Kenny feels like the odd one out, the weird one, the one who's 'just so negative'. He certainly plays that role. Perhaps he does so on behalf of other people as well as himself? Perhaps he represents *their* not knowing as well as his own?

It's true that saying 'I don't know' can be a way of avoiding talking about painful or embarrassing things but most young people say they don't know because they don't. After all, how's Kenny supposed to know why his parents split up? He knows the official story ('My dad started seeing this other woman') but – at 15 – he's old enough to know that there was probably more to it than that. His father won't talk about it, though, while his mother just glares back and says 'Ask your father!' Nor can Kenny find out whether she and her boyfriend are planning to have a baby because it feels too personal, he says, meaning that he'd rather eat Brussels sprouts than think about the possibility of his mother having a sex life!

I don't blame him. No sooner do young people think they know something than they're accused of being cocky and are assured that, at their age, they know nothing at all. And then when they admit that they don't know things, everyone gets upset and tells them that they jolly well *ought* to know!

Not knowing poses problems for counsellors trying to support young people, because when counsellors admit that they don't know the answers *either*, many young people are perturbed. Surely adults are supposed to know? Surely they must have *some* idea? For besieged teachers expected to produce tangible results, not knowing about intangible things is particularly hard. The future is exciting, they insist; learning is exciting; there are so many exciting opportunities and, if you work hard, you'll succeed. Things can only get better!

Kenny has come to see me at the suggestion of these teachers. They want me to fix him up with a sense of purpose, a sense of direction, so that he'll go back to lessons fired up with ambition and self-belief, knowing what's worth doing and how to do it. And the quicker the better.

Phillips (1994) writes that people come to therapy because the story that they've been telling about their lives no longer makes sense. In other words, they find themselves in a state of not knowing (or no longer knowing) what to think about important things like, 'How can the future possibly be exciting when we don't know what's going to happen? When things could go wrong? When we could make mistakes? When we could die?' Or not knowing things like, 'Why did my mum and dad split up, really? Was it all my dad's fault? I remember them arguing. I remember my mum always going off to the pub...'

Kenny doesn't know if he really fancies Charlotte. 'I know I like her,' he says, 'but I don't know if I love her. Trouble is, she keeps asking all the time and, when I say I don't know, she gets all moody like we should break up or something.'

I assure him that not knowing is normal; that we don't know what we think or feel about all sorts of things – often because we have mixed feelings about them – and that when it comes to love, not knowing is usually the truth.

'She wants us to have sex,' he says, 'but I don't know if we should. I mean, I'd *like* to – who wouldn't! – but I don't want to mess her around if we're not going to stay together.'

Not knowing makes young people anxious and, because of this, they clutch at certainties. 'If we have sex,' Charlotte might implicitly be saying to Kenny, 'then that'll prove how much we love each other. We've been going out together for six weeks: surely that proves something! Look at all the presents I've bought you! And what I did to that girl who was flirting with you! Everyone says that we're good together... Of course we love each other! It's obvious!'

Searching for tangible proof to put themselves out of the misery of not knowing, there are young people who end up doing things that can't be undone – getting pregnant, getting married – in order to banish the anxiety of not knowing when everyone else seems to know.

'Mum, how did you and Dad know that you loved each other?'

'We just knew!'

'You mean, because you fancied each other?'

'No, not just that...'

'What then?'

'I don't know! Look, we just knew, okay!'

I remember agreeing with one young person that we'd ban the word 'love' from our counselling conversations as too imprecise, too simplistic. This seemed to help, taking away any pretence of knowing what we meant when – most of the time – we didn't.

Kenny struggles with not knowing what he feels about Charlotte and, as his counsellor, I join him in his struggling, helping him to bear the experience of not knowing, and think about it. There's pressure on me to provide him with certainties yet learning to bear the anxiety of not knowing is at the heart of psychotherapy and at the heart of school life.

'I don't know if I love her,' he says. 'How am I supposed to know?'

I tell him – again – that not knowing is normal.

'So how come nobody else has this problem?'

'Maybe they try to convince themselves that everything is certain because they can't bear to live with uncertainty.'

'Are you saying I should just decide?'

'No, I'm not saying that. I'm saying that your honest truth is that you don't know, Kenny. You can't *pretend* to love someone. That's not fair. When we don't know, we just have to wait and see. And that's a really difficult thing to do but – usually – it's the truth.'

We're better able to bear the anxieties of not knowing when it feels as if our not knowing is understood by another person. This might not seem like much of an achievement in counselling but I think it's the ultimate achievement: one human being understanding another. Feeling understood, our relief is primitive, like a baby's when its cries are finally heard and interpreted correctly. Feeling understood means that we're no longer weird or stupid. Instantly, the world becomes a better place. We relax. I'm not arguing for counsellors to become hapless incompetents, professing to know nothing about anything and never daring to express an opinion. Young people need counsellors who know things and sometimes say what they know; they need counsellors who are wise and can make sense of things when they themselves can't. With young people it's often appropriate to be directive, but young people also need counsellors who don't know, because there are times when not knowing is the simple truth and containment involves bearing those times together, calmly and without panicking. Indeed, Bion (1970) suggests that therapists should strive for 'negative capability', a quality of not knowing first described by the poet John Keats. In rejecting attempts to rationalise away the mysteries of the world, Keats (in a letter written in December 1817) proposed a state of 'Negative Capability, that is, when a man is capable of being in uncertainties, Mysteries, doubts, without any irritable reaching after fact & reason' (in Gittings, 2009, pp.40–1).

The alternative to not knowing is to reach irritably after fact and reason. When young people can't bear not to know, they panic and regress, splitting the world into good things and bad things, into love and hate, truth and lies, us and them. They take refuge in a simpler, childlike world of apparent certainties, and the job of a counsellor is to draw them gently back from that world, supporting them as they try, once more, to bear all the doubts, anxieties and frustrations of life.

There's another anxiety troubling Kenny which, again, is born of not knowing. He's close to his grandmother – his mother's mother – and she has cancer. That much he does know. What he doesn't know (because no one will talk about it) is whether she'll die.

He says the cancer is in her intestines.

I ask whether she's had chemotherapy.

'D'you mean when your hair falls out? Yeah, she had that and she got a wig and everything but her hair never fell out.' Apparently she's feeling better at the moment but Kenny's not convinced. 'She's not the same. She gets tired. She can't go to the shops. She has this woman who comes to help her.'

I ask if he thinks she'll die.

'How would I know? Haven't a clue!'

'Cancer is serious,' I say. 'Hopefully she'll recover but it's always possible that a person with cancer might die because of the illness.'

'You think so?'

I say I've no idea but, yes, it's always possible.

He shakes his head in dismay. 'Fucking stupid!'

'Stupid that people get ill? Stupid that they die?'

'Yeah! Doesn't make sense…'

I agree with him: death doesn't make sense. Perhaps that's the reason we avoid talking about it and particularly avoid talking with young people about it. They think and worry about death far more than adults would like to believe (Luxmoore 2012), and not only do they think about dying physically and what that'll be like, but they think about the fact of life being finite – finite *despite* all that talk about the future, the future, the future and the exciting opportunities waiting for those who work hard. Why bother to do anything when we're going to die anyway?

It's a good question, a really good question. Young people are sometimes fobbed off with answers about the importance of having a family, living the good life, making money, serving God... But more often adults avoid the question of 'Why bother...?' for fear of not having the answer. It's a question that rattles our cages. We feel as if we ought to know, as if we ought to be able to put young people's minds at rest and reassure them that life is worthwhile.

'Why is it worthwhile?'

'Because it is!'

'Yeah, but why?'

It's a question underpinning everything. 'If I'm going to die, then why should I bother to behave? Why should I save my money? Why should I respect other people? Why should I care about the future or revise for my exams?'

Without opportunities to talk about these things and feeling that they should have their own answers, young people's anxieties about death seep out (Luxmoore 2012). They go round trying to look tough and courageous, apparently unafraid. Or they attach desperately, merging with other people in order not to feel alone. They take physical and sexual risks, defying death. They fight with authority-figures because they can't fight with death, the greatest authority-figure of all. Underneath so much of their behaviour they're forever asking why – 'Why do we have to die? Why will I have to die?' – but no one will engage with the question for fear of not being able to provide The Answer.

Not knowing seems to me to be the only emotionally and intellectually honest answer to the question. We don't know why people have to die. We don't know why some people – good people – die before their time. We don't understand the meaning of these things and we spend our lives trying to work it out. In my experience, young people find this admission reassuring. Not knowing is less anxiety-provoking than pretending to know when we don't. As I've said, one of the most important tasks for counsellors is to bear another person's not knowing. Finding someone in school prepared to do this leaves young people feeling less alone; it makes their questioning and not knowing normal rather than mad or foolish or 'just so negative'.

The process of counselling itself provides an opportunity to practise not knowing. It 'weans people from their compulsion to understand and be understood', writes Phillips (2012, p.63), for not only do young people like Kenny not know about love and death but they don't know what's going to happen from week to week in counselling. In counselling they can practise not knowing, entrusting themselves to a process over which they have partial but never complete control. Sometimes the experience will be reassuring and sometimes it'll be disconcerting as meaning is negotiated and re-negotiated, as the circumstances of the young person's life change, as the relationship between the two people in the counselling room becomes closer and as the ending of their relationship approaches.

Still thinking about his grandmother, Kenny looks downcast. 'It's so stupid!'

'Why do you think that some people – good people like your grandmother, Kenny – get cancer?'

He says he doesn't know.

I say I don't know either. 'Like you say, it doesn't make sense.'

He looks at me, still worried but also, I sense, relieved that these things are unclear to other people as well, relieved that there's no right answer and that he's not getting it wrong. Most young people never allow themselves to stay in a relationship where the outcome is unclear and the other person doesn't make everything all right. Counselling is a new experience for Kenny.

Young people's anxieties about not knowing inevitably inform staff anxieties about not knowing and vice versa. Under pressure from governments, schools put huge amounts of energy into planning, predicting and trying to ensure that there will be quantifiable outcomes whenever money is spent on education. The language and practices of business have been adopted in the expectation that a young person's learning and progress can be predicted and monitored through a tight development plan and that the whole process can be evaluated against a set of pre-established criteria.

These processes take no account of contingencies, of the unexpected and unpredictable, of the emergent nature of learning

(Mowles 2011). Development plans defend organisations against the unpredictable, against the things that can't be known and the anxieties of not knowing them. Of course, every teacher knows that planning is essential but they also know that things happen, things go wrong, creative opportunities appear suddenly and the moment has to be seized. After all, young people are growing; the story they tell is constantly changing. A school is an organism with constantly changing dynamics in which the structured and the unstructured co-exist. No sooner is something achieved than new situations arise requiring new responses.

Living with this is tiring. Sometimes it's assumed that those members of staff using the counselling service will be young or new to the school because they're the ones likely to be struggling. But this isn't necessarily the case. In my experience, *all* members of staff struggle with a sense of how things once were and how they are now; with how things are now and how they might be tomorrow; with the fact that, in healthy organisations, there will always be an interplay between the structured and the unstructured, the known and the unknown.

Anil is quickly into it. 'In the past, students respected teachers,' he says. 'It's not like that now! In the old days you were allowed time off when your wife was ill. You'd never hear of that nowadays!' He goes on, describing his struggle with so many things changing. 'The syllabus changes every year! You never have time to consolidate. They're always wanting new schemes of work, new methods of assessment!' The fact that he's 59 years old only makes it harder. Yes, he's seen it all before and knows what to expect, but that doesn't necessarily make it any easier. He's tired, he says, but not old enough to retire.

I agree with him about the frustration of all this. 'You're getting older, Anil...'

'Don't mention that!' he says. 'Next year I'll be 60!'

I ask what it feels like to be nearly 60.

'Do you really want to know? Frightening! I don't know where the time's gone. It doesn't seem to be so long ago that I was one of the young teachers! I'm not complaining – there are good things about being older – but it's not the same. Teaching's not the same.'

'Are you the same?'

'In my heart I'm the same as I've ever been,' he says. 'I'm just – I don't know – *older!*'

'Older and wiser? Older and sadder? Older and angrier?'

'Oh, angrier!' he says at once. 'Much angrier. And I don't know why. I've got no particular reason to be angry. I'm lucky in all sorts of ways. It's just… I don't know. In some ways I can't wait to retire and get out of this hell-hole. But I know that there'll be some things I'll miss.'

Because it's a subject not to be avoided, I ask if he thinks much about death.

'Not really. I tend to think that's years ahead of me and I'll worry about it when the time comes.' He pauses. 'No, I probably do think about it. I suppose we all do in a way. I don't *like* thinking about it, though. I don't like the thought of not knowing what's going to happen…'

For most people, including young people like Kenny, anxieties spoken about are anxieties less likely to be enacted. This matters because Anil is quite capable of taking his anxieties out on students and colleagues by missing days, missing deadlines, sulking. Kenny simply has a different repertoire of anxious behaviours to which other people in school will respond with more behaviour plans, more schemes of work, more assessment criteria: all the initiatives that Anil and Kenny resent but which are essentially the organisation's defences against the anxieties of not knowing.

Part Three

DEVELOPING
THE SERVICE

11
THE HEADTEACHER

Everybody associated with a school has strong feelings about the headteacher because everybody has strong feelings about rules and authority; they have a lifetime's experience of fairness and unfairness which they bring to bear on the person called 'headteacher'. Without opportunities to understand these feelings, the danger is that they get enacted at the headteacher's expense or, indeed, at the expense of the person feeling them. Helping young people and staff think about the headteacher and what he or she represents is often one of a counsellor's tasks.

Sometimes it's simple. 'The head's the worst thing about this school,' says 14-year-old Sophia. 'She makes terrible decisions. Like the one about uniform. And she says she consults us but she never does. She treats us like children who can't be trusted. I've given up! I used to work hard and join in with everything but now I can't be bothered!'

As soon as we get on to talking about her family, it emerges that Sophia feels exactly the same way about her mother. If it wasn't for her mother, everything in Sophia's life would be fine, apparently.

Her mother's bossy and patronising and Sophia's given up on their relationship, she says.

When the moment seems right, I wonder aloud about whether her strong feelings about the headteacher might possibly be fuelled by her feelings about her mother.

She concedes that, yes, that might well be the case. And smiles.

Vera's a caretaker. She's been asked to meet with the headteacher and doesn't know why. Unable to sustain her tough, don't-mess-with-me persona, she's frightened, imagining the worst. 'She and I have never got on,' she says. 'She criticises everything I do. The other night I was putting out chairs for the concert and she came in and said that the front row was too near. And as you know, this school's making cuts, so you can guess who'll be the first to lose their job!'

It sounds highly unlikely that the headteacher would want to make one of the caretakers redundant because the chairs in the front row of the audience were too near to the musicians. But Vera's upset.

'Have you ever met anyone like her before?' I ask. 'Does she remind you of anyone?'

Immediately she gets it. 'My father!' she says. 'I was always scared of him and he *did* always criticise me! I was always expecting to be told off!' She marvels at the connection. 'That's it! That's why it gets to me! That's why I always imagine the worst!'

A week later, she finds me to tell me that she did meet with the headteacher who, far from making her redundant, was asking whether she'd take on extra responsibilities for more money.

Counsellors take these unconscious connections for granted. Of course our strong feelings nowadays are likely to be informed by experiences earlier in our lives. But this isn't obvious to everyone. There are all sorts of learnings from psychotherapy to be disseminated in a school as long as the counsellor can do this in a way that isn't patronising or self-congratulatory. At the school where I work, I edit a termly magazine for staff, getting colleagues to write about their work and share their thinking with each other (see Chapter 7). The magazine also allows me to write occasional pieces myself, highlighting and reflecting on various issues. For one edition, I wrote the following:

THERE'S NO SUCH THING AS A HEADTEACHER

Headteachers exist in the eye of the beholder. In fact, we all exist in the eye of the beholder in the sense that we exist when other people see us and confirm our existence, giving us an identity. We might see ourselves as hard-working but if another person sees us as lazy then that's who we are in their eyes. Another person might see us as stubborn or hilarious or kind. We become different people according to who's describing us, and so, if there are 300 members of staff in a school, there'll be 300 different headteachers.·

I'm exaggerating. Of course a headteacher has an objective existence as well. Everyone recognises the person in smart clothes walking down the corridor, 'Here comes the headteacher!' It's just that this same headteacher also exists subjectively for us all and so the person we see in the corridor – the person whom we greet smilingly or whom we choose to ignore – will be a different person for us all. Because of the role, headteachers become parent-figures in our heads but the kind of parent-figure will be different for everyone. Our personal sense of the 'headteacher' will depend on the many experiences of parenting we carry inside us: experiences of feeling valued or unvalued in our lives, loved or unloved, admired or scorned by parents and other important authority-figures.

The danger of this is that, if we're not careful, we end up thinking about and reacting to the person in the corridor as if he or she is the one in our heads. I've been in staff meetings in schools where the headteacher has been accused of saying or doing or being things which (to my mind) have had nothing whatsoever to do with that headteacher's particular stance on something but have said much more about the person making the accusation, about his or her sense of mattering, of being taken seriously, of feeling valued and respected in the world.

We all have some inkling of what it's like to be the headteacher. As authority-figures and parent-figures ourselves, we've all been on the receiving end of other people's projections. We all know what it's like to be treated as something we're not and to find ourselves thinking, 'Whoa! Where did that come from? I didn't deserve that!' We know how we tend to react on these occasions. Headteachers are no different. Knowing that they'll never be able to please all of the people all of the time, some become paralysed by so many powerful projections and unable to act. Others react impulsively, unleashing their own subjectivities as they reward and punish indiscriminately, taking revenge. But the best headteachers seem to find a way of understanding and forgiving the projections coming their way, knowing that – for the most part – they're not as personal as they feel but are about the many things that a headteacher represents.

Of course there's always an objective reality: a headteacher is a person with likes and dislikes, strengths and weaknesses, managing other people with likes and dislikes, strengths and weaknesses. My point is simply that this objective reality is always informed by a subjective one because we can't help bringing our unconscious lives into school with us. Knowing that this is going on allows us to be a little more considered in our judgements.

My intention with this article was to express what I thought was an unspoken, institutional anxiety in the hope of detoxifying its power. If we understand our feelings about the headteacher, we're better able to distinguish between what we bring unconsciously to the relationship and what the headteacher brings.

Like Sophia the student and Vera the caretaker, 13-year-old Elsie's feelings about her male headteacher are related to her feelings about her parents. She swears at him and gets herself excluded from school. She does it again. She gets excluded again. She understands perfectly well that it's what he represents rather than the man himself. She understands that – really – she's fighting with her parents and that getting excluded is a way of getting their attention. Yet despite these understandings, she's still drawn into some kind of confrontation with the headteacher whenever she sees him.

What's hard for her to understand or admit is her *need* for him. Fighting him is actually a way of having a relationship with him. Fighting him, she gets to spend time in his office and, because of this, he always says hello when he sees her. In fact, he becomes especially interested in her progress. Fighting is an expression of her need to be loved by this man in a suit.

'He means a lot to you, Elsie.'

'Wrong! He means nothing to me!'

'What I mean is that you've got strong feelings about him.'

'Certainly have!'

'You hate him. You fight with him. You never give him a moment's peace. You're always in his office. In a funny kind of way, you're quite close to each other. You're both stubborn. Both determined. Both care passionately. Both believe in fairness.'

She thinks about this. 'Funnily enough,' she says, 'the other day he said he didn't agree with me but he respected me.'

I ask what that was like to hear.

'Quite good, really. Shows he's not completely dumb!'

'Shows he cares?'

'Maybe...'

'Cares about you?'

'Doubt that,' she says. And quickly changes the subject.

But we've touched on what's hardest for her to acknowledge – her need for this man everybody talks about, this man who's roughly the same age as her parents. She needs him but can't tell him. And of course her need is transferred onto him from her underlying need for her parents. We begin what will be many hours of talking about *them* – the sadness and hurt, the feeling that she's losing them, disappointing them – and their seeming inability to understand that their teenage daughter *hasn't* suddenly become the devil incarnate. Because Elsie finds her relationships at home painful and complicated, she tries to reduce all her relationships to mechanical battles about rules.

Amongst her friends, the headteacher is the object of constant criticism. Swearing about him behind his back is like repeating the group password. And in the staffroom the headteacher is also the object, if not of constant criticism, then of constant speculation. What's he thinking? What's he planning? Who's in his good books? Who's not? For some, every moment of contact with the headteacher is experienced as a slight or as tacit approval.

Whenever we meet, Patrick supplies me with the latest staffroom gossip and speculation. He can't help himself. Without any of Elsie's truculence, this talented professional is reduced to a similar obsession. He never feels sufficiently recognised by the headteacher. He thinks other members of staff get more praise and are held in higher esteem by the headteacher. He thinks they're more likely to get promoted by the headteacher while his own efforts will be taken for granted. Like other members of staff, he sees himself as the glue holding the school together but never getting the recognition that he deserves.

Patrick was adopted by loving parents but admits that a part of him has never felt satisfied. It's as if his adoptive parents' love was never enough; as if something was always missing. And he agrees that – unconsciously – he probably can't help looking to his male headteacher for the kind of recognition that the man in the suit will never be able to give him. He thinks about resigning because then – in Patrick's fantasy – the school will fall apart. *Then* they'll realise! *Then* they'll be sorry! I encourage him to talk to the headteacher about his future at the school and, when he does, he's partially satisfied. Partially. Despite his understanding of what the headteacher represents for him, it's still hard to accept that this man, this headteacher is a person like anyone else with his own limitations, his own needs, his own family: another person like Patrick, doing his best, muddling through.

The conversation that Patrick really needs to have is with the parents who gave him up for adoption. He's never met them or tried to trace them but, in his head, has always been asking them questions... 'Why did you do it? Was there something wrong with me? How could you have been so selfish? Why didn't you love me?' or possibly, as I suggest to him, 'Did you love me *so much* that you had me adopted so that I could have a better life?'

'I've thought of that,' he says. 'But if I had a kid, I could never give him away. I'd always want to be there for him.'

'Maybe you would,' I say, 'but neither of us knows what it's like to have no money or to be scared stiff or to be addicted to drugs or to have no partner or to be pregnant by accident. It's hard for us to know what any of that would be like if it happened to us.'

He thinks about this.

'I imagine that your birth mother would be very proud of you,' I say. 'Very proud and very sad.'

His eyes glisten.

'And in school, no one will ever know about how sad it is for you sometimes, working so hard for your students and loving them when sometimes you don't feel loved yourself. They'll never know how unfair that feels or how much it hurts.'

There's a long pause.

He sighs deeply. 'Guess I'll just have to get on with it!'

'You will. And it'll always be sad and always unfair and our poor old headteacher will never be able to change that!'

There's always a reason why the most passionate, committed teachers like Patrick do their jobs; why they choose to work with sometimes unhappy, sometimes disturbed young people; why they choose to work as part of a staff team they sometimes describe as being like a family. It's about more than money and holidays. As Obholzer and Zagier Roberts (1994) write, 'The choices we make regarding which profession to train for, which client group we will work with, and in what kind of setting, are all profoundly influenced by our need to come to terms with unresolved issues from our past' (p.110). Teachers become parent figures because they have strong feelings about parent figures. They can't help having strong feelings about the headteacher, therefore, and, for many, that means needing his recognition and approval.

But as a person like any other person, who does the headteacher get his or her own recognition and approval from? In Chapter 2, I described one way in which a counsellor's relationship with the headteacher might typically begin. But how might it develop? How might a counsellor become a support to the headteacher without taking sides? Our capacity to offer other people recognition and approval depends on the extent to which we feel recognised and approved of ourselves; our tendency to criticise and denigrate depends on the extent to which we feel criticised and denigrated ourselves.

Knowing that the counsellor is being told all sorts of things by people like Sophia, Vera, Elsie and Patrick, headteachers sense whether or not the counsellor takes their stories at face value and disapproves, or understands that there's always more to a situation than meets the eye. They sense whether the counsellor understands that the headteacher is trying his or her absolute best in difficult circumstances, faced with the projections of Sophia, Vera, Elsie and Patrick, not to mention the projections of parents, journalists, politicians and everyone else for whom the words 'headteacher' and 'school' immediately provoke strong feelings (Luxmoore 2008).

Headteachers are the same as counsellors in that they tend to approve of people who approve of them. In the schools where I've worked as the counsellor, I may have disagreed with the headteacher in private but in public I've always tried to express my admiration for the things that he or she is doing well in difficult circumstances. This has to be the starting point. An outraged counsellor charging into a headteacher's office to defend a student about to be excluded is asking for trouble. Sometimes students *have* to be excluded (rules have to be enforced) and usually the headteacher has no choice. There might well be ways of letting her know how difficult things are at home for the student (assuming that she doesn't already know) but the counsellor has to work with rather than against the pragmatic realities of school life. A few days' exclusion probably won't help the student any more than going to prison will help the offender, but it'll help the school if it reminds everyone that certain behaviours aren't tolerated. The brutal fact is that sometimes things have to be done for the greater good.

Because most headteachers imagine that counsellors are softies who'll automatically take the side of young people, it's encouraging to know that your school counsellor *does* understand that other things have to be taken into account, however unfortunate a young person's circumstances may be. I'm not suggesting that headteachers never make mistakes: of course there are some who use rules to defend themselves against relationships; there are some who use their power to take revenge, and there are some who unconsciously enact their own life stories, trying to get their own needs met at the expense of other people. But counsellors are no different: they're just luckier. Counsellors can meet regularly with a supervisor in order to make sense of things, potentially disentangling their own needs from those of other people and potentially seeing things more clearly as a result. Headteachers have much more pressure on them than counsellors. Every week, they must manage *hundreds* rather than dozens of relationships and, to help them do this, they get no supervision at all. (One of the reasons why headteachers are sometimes reluctant to pay for a counsellor's supervision might be because they never get any themselves.) A few headteachers set something up for themselves – some non-managerial mechanism which gives them space in which to think – but most soldier on, too busy to make time to reflect, worrying that doubt or uncertainty of any kind will be unproductive.

The closest they come to what counsellors call 'supervision' might be with their own school counsellor. If the counsellor clearly respects the difficulty of the headteacher's job; if she's earned her credibility by working at the school for longer than five minutes and has been willing to get her hands dirty; if she clearly doesn't take sides… If all of these things are in place then maybe, just *maybe* the headteacher might use the counsellor for supervision. It won't be formal and it won't have a name. It certainly won't be called 'supervision' but that's what it'll be, in effect. And it'll be occasioned by remarks like 'I just need to pick your brains about something' or 'Have you got time for a quick chat?' or, simply, 'How are you doing?', meaning, 'I'd like to tell you how *I'm* doing…'

The counsellor listens, wonders aloud, listens some more, agrees that there's no right answer and that being a headteacher is tough. Occasionally there are insights to be offered – the possibility of people having mixed feelings, of feelings from childhood being acted out by staff and parents – but often the job is to be with the headteacher in the face of his or her unpopularity, of so many no-win situations, of teacher-children squabbling in the staffroom and the headteacher-parent in his or her office, longing to give them a verbal slap.

12
VOLUNTEER COUNSELLORS

'Of course, it would be lovely to have more counsellors,' says the headteacher, 'but we just don't have the money at the moment!'

Once young people and staff begin to trust and value the counselling service, they want more of it. Increasingly, young people will be referring themselves for counselling and more and more parents will be asking if their child can see a counsellor. One of my solutions to the problem of capacity has been to recruit a team of volunteers: counsellors towards the end of their training or established counsellors wanting more experience of young people and school settings. I supervise each counsellor who, in return for an hour's supervision a fortnight, will typically be seeing six young people.

Because credibility is all, it's important that these volunteers are good enough as clinicians. So I meet with prospective volunteers informally to tell them about the counselling service and hear about their experience. If that goes well, we progress to a formal interview a few weeks later. This interview has to be rigorous because, if appointed, the counsellor will become a de facto member of staff, responsible for other people's children.

At least one other member of staff joins me in the interview. This matters because the staff as a whole will have part-ownership of whomsoever we appoint. They'll be working with this volunteer, trusting her with 'their' students. Joining us in the interview are at least two young people who've had counselling themselves or who are still using the counselling service. For them, this is an opportunity to think about the processes of counselling and see themselves from the counsellor's chair. When it's their turn, they ask the volunteer set questions, chipping in with supplementary questions and listening as the volunteer reacts to an unfolding case study.

Our most important task is to discover what this person might be like as a clinician. Already the volunteer knows that I believe in an integrated, whole-school counselling service so it's easy to answer questions about the place of counselling in a school. It's the case study which indicates how the interviewee might perform, alone in a counselling room with an anxious young person. What can the counsellor offer beyond listening and empathising? What sense does she have of young people's defences, of where the therapy might need to go?

We give the case study to the interviewee, a paragraph at a time, inviting her to think aloud as she gets more and more information. Cross-references and themes emerge as well as practical considerations. For example, we might give the volunteer the following first paragraph:

> One of the senior teachers leaves you a message. She wants you to see Adam, who's 14. Adam's been in a lot of trouble at school – bullying, being rude to teachers, stealing. He's recently been excluded and a condition of coming back to school is that he starts counselling, which he's said he's prepared to do.

We invite the volunteer to read this paragraph and think aloud. A second paragraph then follows with the same invitation to think aloud:

Adam sits down for his first session and says he can't see what all the fuss is about. 'I just don't get on with teachers!'

The volunteer responds before being given a third, short paragraph:

After a silence, Adam asks, 'How exactly is this going to help me?'

Again, the volunteer responds. There's a fourth paragraph:

It emerges that his father left before Adam was born. Adam's mother married his step-father when Adam was three. His step-father was never really interested in Adam, who was always close to his grandmother and spent a lot of time at her house. His mother and step-father divorced when Adam was eleven.

A fifth paragraph:

For the last two years, his mother has had a live-in boyfriend, John. They have a one-year-old son. Adam says he used to get on really well with John but John is rarely at home now since he started working as a long-distance driver. Adam's school work has been getting worse for ages, Adam says. Because of John being away so much, his mother and John might be going to split up.

A sixth paragraph:

Recently, Adam hasn't been seeing so much of his grandmother. When he sees her, he doesn't feel like talking, he says, and that just makes her angry. She accuses him of taking drugs.

A seventh paragraph:

After agreeing to come again, Adam doesn't arrive for his next appointment.

And a final, eighth paragraph:

The Head of Year stops you to ask whether there's anything she and the other teachers should know in order to help Adam.

By the end of the case study, the volunteer's ability to think clearly on different levels while under pressure will be evident. She may say something useful about the role of father figures in Adam's life but have nothing to say about what it's like being a 14-year-old boy in the first place. She may pick up on Adam's transference to teachers but have little idea of how to explain counselling to him. She may be good on his experience of attachment and loss but weak on any mixed feelings he might have as a result. She may suggest that his feelings towards his mother will be complicated but have no thoughts as to why he might not have turned up for a second appointment. She may be very clear about confidentiality but get into a muddle at the thought of working alongside teachers.

Our questioning done, the volunteer goes out of the room and we share our thoughts. The young people are usually remarkably shrewd in their assessments. Inevitably, they'll sympathise with elements of Adam's story, so hearing the volunteer think aloud about him gives them insights into how their own counsellor might think about them and, potentially, this helps them to think about themselves.

Once appointed, volunteer counsellors build up their caseload as they build up their confidence. They learn about adapting to young people and to the demands of the institution. They make friends with the receptionists. They brave the staffroom. They go into classrooms sensitively and fetch students who've forgotten appointments. They find ways of talking with members of staff without compromising anyone's confidentiality. Sometimes they make mistakes – sticking rigidly to an approach better suited to adults, for example, or involving themselves in the minutiae of a student's school life. Sometimes they miss things, concentrating on a young person's drug-taking, for example, while ignoring the feelings it might be concealing. They panic sometimes. They get angry. They get scared. As long as they bring these things to supervision, we can move forward together.

13
PEER SUPPORTERS

We sit in a circle. Each person takes a turn to report back on his or her work with younger students during the past fortnight: the progress of the boy who was friendless at the start of the year, the difficulties of dealing with a clinging girl, the delights of running group warm-up exercises with a tutor group, the dilemmas of how to respond to sexual comments, the concern about a group of girls who've fallen out with each other, the relief that a planned meeting with a particularly vulnerable student went well, the satisfaction of adapting a group exercise so that the whole class could join in, the issue of how much personal information to disclose, the pleasure when so many younger students are so keen to chat, the courage to be firm with disruptive students and the understanding that, underneath their behaviour, these students are anxious... As usual, I'm touched by the compassion of the peer supporters and by their level of insight.

Different schools use different names. Some call them 'buddies' or 'befrienders', 'student counsellors', 'peer mentors' or 'peer listeners'. I call them 'peer supporters', although that's a misnomer because, strictly speaking, they're not peers. In most schools, they're older students whose job is to support younger students, the way older siblings might support younger siblings (Luxmoore 2000), demonstrating that support isn't something offered only by counsellors and other members of staff, but is the concern of everyone – adults and young people alike.

For the past 26 years, I've trained teams of peer supporters in many schools and have managed teams myself. Always the peer supporters have wonderful potential: they're kind, sincere, empathic and emotionally intelligent. The hard bit is sustaining the work once the novelty of the job has worn off. There are schools who launch their peer supporters with a fanfare of training and good wishes, then leave the students to get on with it in the belief that this will be 'empowering' and will be an example of young people 'taking responsibility themselves'. Things quickly fall apart because, for all their potential, the peer supporters are only as good as the way in which they're managed. They may appear effortlessly to spread balm and bonhomie but that rarely happens by accident. It happens because there are structures holding the team together, ensuring that people continue working hard and learning, long after the novelty of the job has worn off.

A well-organised team of peer supporters will probably have filled out an application form before being interviewed and chosen for the job. They'll have been given a job description, spelling out their responsibilities and making their commitment clear. As part of that commitment, they'll be obliged to attend regular team meetings and will be told to expect stern words and sackings, if necessary, should they fail to maintain their commitment. 'The job's too important to do badly,' I explain to the teams I manage. 'I'd rather have a small but fully committed team than a large team whose commitment is uncertain, however talented certain members of the team may be. It's not fair on younger students who've experienced broken attachments and broken promises in their lives to invite attachments and make promises only to let those students down.'

A job description helps to structure the work, yet the most important activity listed in the job description is the most unstructured. 'Creative loitering' is the glue that holds everything together, allowing the peer supporters to make and maintain relationships with younger students. I've known schools where a team of well-meaning peer supporters is trained to staff a room at lunchtime where younger students can come in and talk about their concerns. Enthusiastically, the team puts up posters around school advertising the room. They speak to assemblies. They devise a rota and, when it's their turn to be in the lunchtime room, they set up chairs, put on background music and wait for younger students to come flooding in.

Nothing happens.

They put up fresh posters. They ask the teachers to remind everyone about the existence of the room.

Still nothing happens. No one uses the room because no one knows the people inside it. Younger students will only use the privacy of a lunchtime room once they've got to know and begun to trust the people inside it. And that's where 'creative loitering' is the part of the job from which everything else proceeds. It's the skill of wandering around school, apparently minding one's own business but always looking to smile at people, always looking to say hello and pick up conversations, gradually getting to know dozens of younger students by name, always pleased to see them, remembering things about them, enjoying their company... And *then* out of these informal, daily conversations, other conversations emerge that are more personal, more serious, more urgent. But these conversations only emerge once a relationship with a peer supporter is established. 'You're a peer supporter from the moment you walk into school until the moment you walk out,' I tell my teams. 'In fact, you're a peer supporter out of school as well, because you can't ignore someone in the supermarket just because you're no longer on school premises. Wherever you go, you're on duty. You may not always have time to stop and talk but you'll always say hello. Wherever you go, you'll always be pleased to see younger students.'

Some peer supporters take to creative loitering like ducks to water while others need more encouragement. In some cases, I watch the reluctant loiterers and suggest ways of doing it differently. Or I demonstrate it myself and get them to try. Knowing that getting better at it is the only option, they relax eventually and, after a few months, creative loitering becomes a pleasure.

The effect of these informal relationships, this daily drip-feed of conversation, contributes powerfully to the culture of a school, breaking down the often ruinous hierarchies between age groups. The peer supporters are modelling a concern for others which potentially rubs off on everyone. When older students are friendly and kind, why wouldn't younger students also be friendly and kind? When older students are interested in younger students, why wouldn't those younger students be interested in each other? Well-managed peer supporters will do good work with specific individuals and groups, but their greater contribution to a school will be subversive, making it normal for friendly relationships to be happening everywhere, regardless of age and other differences between people.

Like all the peer supporters, Lotus is attached to a tutor group of younger students. She worries that the relationships she has with them aren't as close as the relationships other members of the team seem to have with their tutor groups. At our team meeting, we remind her that, because she was ill, she missed the vital first day of the school year when the younger students were all shiny and new, looking to make attachments. We conclude that it's going to take her a while to catch up. We agree that boys can be harder to talk with than girls and I remind the team of how discombobulating it can be for a 12-year-old boy to find himself talking to a glamorous older student *with breasts!*

Different schools deploy their peer supporters in different ways and use different age groups as peer supporters. Some schools recruit the more academically able or better-behaved students as peer supporters. Other schools deliberately recruit students who have been through tough times themselves (Luxmoore 2010). What matters more than their age or behavioural history is how they're managed. I've been to train peer supporters in schools where – before the work has even begun – the rot has set in: the way in which the peer supporters were recruited was haphazard; there was a meeting that no one knew about; two peer supporters have already managed to exempt themselves from some of the training; one student has been allowed to join the team late and, even as the training starts, the team's exact duties are still being decided by senior teachers…

Already, the message is that this initiative is a muddle. The peer supporters will do their best once they start work but the initiative quickly breaks down because precedents have been set. Team cohesion has already been undermined. As I've described elsewhere (Luxmoore 2000), the lookers-after must themselves feel looked after or they lose heart. The training is easy: we can practise creative loitering; we can practise listening skills; we can practise for specific situations; we can come together as a team and agree all sorts of practical arrangements long before anyone starts any face-to-face work with younger students. We can get off to a good start with everyone organised and clear about what they're doing. That's the easy bit. The hard bit comes later.

Brigid misses a team meeting without sending her apologies or any message. A bad precedent will be set unless I tackle her firmly and unless the rest of the team finds out that she didn't get away with it. I seek her out.

She explains that she was behind with her coursework.

I remind her of the line in the job description about peer supporters keeping up with their schoolwork so that it doesn't interfere with their peer support work.

She says that her parents told her to get the coursework done rather than come to the meeting.

I tell her that I don't want to lose her from the team but that this can't happen again; that she'll have to resign from the team if she finds herself unable to manage both commitments.

She's a very good peer supporter and doesn't want to resign, and it's rare for peer supporters to use coursework as an excuse. But the rest of the team also have coursework to do and will be keen to know what happened with Brigid. I tell her that, at our next team meeting, I'll be explaining to the others why she missed the meeting and that it won't be happening again.

She can hear that I mean it and looks askance, surprised that the nice school counsellor has this side to him, little knowing that – without this side – most peer supporter teams disintegrate.

Alan reports that the students he got to know at the beginning of the year don't seem to need him any longer. 'They've all made friends,' he says. 'They seem quite happy to get on without me.'

Other members of the team aren't so certain. 'Mine made friends at the beginning,' reports Mikey, 'and now they're all falling out with each other. I had two boys threatening to fight each other last week and two girls coming up to me in tears because they'd just broken friends!'

I explain to Alan and the team that people's needs change. 'They don't need you any more or less than they did at the beginning of term. They just need you differently. New things are happening: things like sex and sexuality, boyfriends and girlfriends, making new friends and jettisoning old ones, worrying about how they look, stuff going on at home...'

Merita tells us about a girl she's got to know whose parents are splitting up. 'I didn't know what to say,' she tells us. 'I didn't want to make anything worse...'

Luke says that he's stopped worrying about giving the wrong advice. 'They just want you to listen,' he says to Merita. 'There's nothing you *can* say, really.'

I agree with him. I encourage them all – now that their relationships are established – to seek opportunities for longer conversations. 'When someone tells you something important like the fact that their parents are splitting up, you probably won't have time to talk about it properly then and there, but you can arrange to see them at another time in the week.'

Clayton says he's done this once or twice, 'And it wasn't as bad as I thought. In fact, I hardly had to say anything. The boy just talked. And then, at the end, he got up and thanked me!'

It's vital that the peer supporters stay together as a team and don't split off into factions. Our team meetings serve partly as ways of demystifying members of the team to each other, ways of answering the perennial questions 'Are the others more popular than I am? Are they getting to know more students than I am? Are they better listeners than I am?'

Just as younger students' needs change during a typical year, so the peer supporters' needs change. Once there's a degree of self-confidence in the team, it's important that they keep learning new things and never stagnate. As the year goes on, I teach them new exercises to run with groups (Luxmoore 2002) and they start sharing with each other groupwork exercises that they've developed themselves or remembered from when they were younger. We spend a lot of time thinking about individual students, about what's going on behind the façades, about developmental changes, family systems. I share with them bits of psychotherapy theory. Officially, we're always talking about younger students but the peer supporters are also making sense of themselves, wondering how they fit into this particular theory or relate to that particular experience. They have an agenda beyond altruism: they're interested in proving something important about their capacity to care for other people (Luxmoore 2000).

From time to time, we invite key members of staff to our team meetings, ostensibly to discuss particular students. But these occasions also help to ensure that there are no rifts between the peer supporters and members of staff. Enshrined in the peer supporters' job description is a phrase about 'never undermining the aims of the school or the work of the staff'. This matters because there's the potential for staff to feel jealous when students are confiding in peer supporters rather than in them and there's the potential for some peer supporters to start feeling superior because of their popularity.

In a good school, everyone supports everyone. What turns this bland statement into a reality is the fact that staff *as well as* peer supporters *as well as* counsellors and others are all involved: all with different levels of competence, maybe, but without rivalry. Supporting others is never the sole preserve of counsellors. Or teachers. Or peer supporters.

14
PARENTS

Parents are there all the time in the background: critical, supportive, worried, grateful, desperate. They feature in almost all the stories told in counselling and, like young people and staff, they also have an effect on how a school operates.

Because of this, some school counsellors do a lot of work with parents, arguing that it's at least as important as the work they do with young people. As Hinshelwood (2001) writes, 'The individual originates in an institution' (p.81), and that institution is a family. Family therapists would argue that it's impossible to treat the individual without treating the family of which he or she is a part. So I do some work with parents but never as much as I'd like to do. If they ring, I speak with them on the phone; I see them if they want to meet; I write a monthly column for their newsletter; and, occasionally, I run evening workshops for them exploring some particular aspect of adolescence.

What I've learned is that most parents are very keen to read about parenting, provided that the author understands just how difficult it is to be a parent. I've learned that, whatever pearls of wisdom I may have to impart in workshops, parents remember little of that stuff. What they take from the workshop is the relief of discovering that other parents have the same dilemmas and that their own children – for all their ups and downs – sound relatively normal. I've learned that many parents struggle with the teenager inside themselves and with all the unfinished business from their own teenage years; that most are still struggling with their own parents: the ones they carry around unconsciously in their heads and the ones they visit at weekends.

I respond in these ways but rarely initiate contact with parents myself. I avoid inter-agency meetings where parents are expected to sit and discuss their son's or daughter's behaviour. I'm wary of getting enmeshed in the details of the incident in school last week and the resulting plan of action agreed between the parents and the professionals. Parents care passionately about their children but, like any of us, they only tell one side of the story. Vital bits of information are sometimes left out or avoided in meetings, like the fact that one parent has a drink problem or that the other parent had an affair last year or that their son or daughter is actually adopted. 'Sorry, but we didn't think it was important,' they say when that information emerges, weeks later. Unpicking all this takes time and so – instead of doing lots of casework with parents – I confine myself to working with the young person in the belief that an adjustment to his or her view of the world may well have a knock-on effect on the family system.

However, the school counsellor is always a potential threat to parents ('I'm sure he tells you far more in school than he ever tells us!') and so the counselling service has to be demystified for parents as it does for students and staff. I have a section on the school website and a leaflet for all parents new to the school, explaining what the service is and isn't:

> The Counselling Service is based on the belief that we learn best when we are at ease with ourselves and the world; when we feel confident, secure and valued. All sorts of things can interrupt and impede our learning. Sometimes people in our lives make us feel sad or angry, nervous or useless. Counselling is a chance to talk about these things with someone who is trained, in order to begin to change the way we feel about ourselves and behave towards others.

After describing different aspects of the service, how it works and the people involved, the leaflet ends:

> It's important to remember that the Counselling Service doesn't take the place of parents, friends or form tutors. Indeed, it respects very much the contributions that all these people make in our lives. Counselling isn't a magic solution. The Service does, however, provide an additional, unique kind of support and, as such, plays a vital part in the life of the school.

Because the Counselling Service does play a vital part in the life of the school and isn't secretive about its work, it goes without saying that I don't ask parents for their permission when a young person starts counselling. The message to parents is clear: counselling is a normal activity, not a furtive one; lots of people use the service, including staff, so why wouldn't your son or daughter want to take advantage of an extra kind of support?

Part Four

LIFE AFTER SCHOOL COUNSELLING

15
WHAT
HAPPENS NEXT

What becomes of school counsellors? Do they move on to other schools and start all over again? Do they grow old gracefully? Do they get fed up?

Having settled into her school, the counsellor I described in Chapter 2 might stay for eight months, eight years or 18 years. She might increase or cut back her hours. A new regime might take over at the school, demanding that she explains and justifies her work all over again. She might find herself marginalised by this new regime or given a higher-profile role. She might start training in some other field of psychotherapy, adding new skills to her repertoire, or she might decide to leave the school and do something completely different.

'I've been thinking about my future,' she says to the headteacher at one of their regular meetings.

'You're not leaving?'

'No, I'm not leaving. I'm just wondering what to do next. I've been here for eight years...'

He looks confused. 'There's no shortage of people wanting your services!'

'I know,' she says, 'and if I ever did leave, I wouldn't leave anyone in the lurch. No, it's not that. In a way, I'd be quite happy to continue doing this job for another ten years, but – even so – I've been wondering about it and wondering what to do next. You don't mind me mentioning it, do you?'

'Of course not,' he says. 'To my shame, I've never really thought about you leaving. You've always been a part of what makes this place tick. So I'm afraid I've no idea! What *do* school counsellors do next?'

'There's no pattern,' she explains. 'Some get different jobs. Some work privately, seeing people at home. Some retire.'

'We'd miss you terribly,' he says. 'I hope you won't be leaving just yet!'

'Like I say, I've got no plans,' she assures him. 'I'm not secretly burning with ruthless ambition! I'm just thinking about it, that's all.'

He looks thoughtful. 'I suppose I've sometimes wondered what it must be like, listening to people's problems all the time. I'm aware that we don't listen to yours very often. We just sort of expect you to get on with everything and manage!'

'The job's fine,' she assures him. 'Okay, it has its ups and downs but it's no more stressful than any other job. I'm probably just feeling a bit jaded at the moment.'

He looks at her. 'I've explained the money situation to you, haven't I? If there was money to pay you more, we would. But unfortunately there isn't any at the moment and I'm afraid there's nothing I can do about that.'

'I know,' she says, irritated. 'It's not about money. More money would be nice. But no, this is more about how I want to spend the rest of my working life.'

'Should we be looking at your job description?'

'Not really,' she says. 'I don't think there's much that can be changed. I'm stretched, but probably no more than anyone else these days!'

He looks perplexed, uncomfortable. 'I'm not really sure how I can help...'

'Maybe you can't,' she says. 'Maybe I just have to keep thinking things through for myself.'

He tries to be helpful. 'You must say if there's anything we can do practically. For example, if there are courses you'd like to go on, just ask. Like I say, we don't want to lose you. You know how much I value your work. And the rest of the staff would agree with me. Not to mention all the people you counsel!'

'It's kind of you to say that,' she says. 'I do go on courses occasionally. And I do know that people value the service... Maybe I just needed to mention it here to remind myself that it's something I *am* actually thinking about!'

'Well, to be honest with you,' muses the headteacher, looking out of the window, 'the fact is that none of us will be here forever...'

At this point, the conversation either moves on to his own career dilemmas or reverts to the topics that he and the counsellor usually discuss in their meetings.

When it's time to go, the counsellor gets up, reminded of what she always knew but was somehow hoping might not be true: that the rest of her working life is her responsibility. Headteachers might be able to help plot the careers of teachers but not of school counsellors. In return for the satisfactions of the job, school counsellors give up the possibility of conventional career advancement. They live with exactly the same questions besetting so many people who visit their rooms – 'What am I doing here? What happens next? Where's my life going?' – exciting, difficult questions which counsellors are no better able to answer than anyone else.

'Did you talk to the Head?' the counsellor's supervisor asks at their next meeting. 'What did he say?'

'What I expected him to say,' says the counsellor. 'There was nothing he *could* say, really. It's up to me.'

Her supervisor is well aware of the circumstances of the counsellor's life. Together they wonder whether her restlessness at work is an expression of other issues. They wonder whether she's feeling restless on behalf of her clients, internalising their restlessness as her own. They wonder whether there's a restlessness in the school as a whole which she's somehow picking up… None of these enquiries seems particularly fruitful.

'Perhaps the fact is that, as counsellors, we're no different from anyone else,' her supervisor says, 'except that people keep coming to us expecting wisdom! And we *are* wise in some ways and *do* help and we get used to playing this role for other people. So perhaps it comes as a bit of a shock when all that experience and wisdom seems to have no bearing on our own lives! Perhaps it's a reminder that we're actually no better or wiser or different from anyone else. We're just mucky little humans, muddling through, doing our best!'

'I know that,' the counsellor says, sighing long and hard. 'You're right, of course. The trouble is that you're always bloody right!'

They both laugh.

REFERENCES

Alvarez, A. (1992) *Live Company: Psychoanalytic Psychotherapy with Autistic, Borderline, Deprived and Abused Children.* London and New York, NY: Tavistock/Routledge.

Beebe, B., Jaffe, J., Markese, S., Buck, K. *et al.* (2010) 'The origins of 12-month attachment: A microanalysis of 4-month mother-infant interaction.' *Attachment and Human Development 12*, 1–2, 3–141.

Bion, W. (1961) *Experiences in Groups.* London: Tavistock Publications.

Bion, W. (1963) *Elements of Psycho-Analysis.* London: William Heinemann.

Bion, W. (1970) *Attention and Interpretation.* London: Tavistock Publications.

Bramley, W. (1996) *The Supervisory Couple in Broad-Spectrum Psychotherapy.* London: Free Association Books.

Davies, J. (2012) *The Importance of Suffering: The Value and Meaning of Emotional Discontent.* London: Routledge.

Fonagy, P., Gergely, G., Jurist, E.J. and Target, M. (2004) *Affect Regulation, Mentalization, and the Development of the Self.* London: Karnac Books.

Foulkes, S.H. (1948) *Introduction to Group Analytic Psychotherapy.* London: Heinemann.

Gerhardt, S. (2004) *Why Love Matters: How Affection Shapes a Baby's Brain.* Hove: Brunner-Routledge.

Gittings, R. (ed.) (2009) *John Keats: Selected Letters.* Oxford: Oxford University Press.

Glasser, M. (1979) 'Some Aspects of the Role of Aggression in the Perversions.' In I. Rosen (ed.) *Sexual Deviation.* Oxford, New York, NY, and Toronto: Oxford University Press.

Halton, W. (1994) 'Some Unconscious Aspects of Organisational Life: Contributions from Psychoanalysis.' In A. Obholzer and V. Zagier Roberts (eds) *The Unconscious at Work*. London: Routledge.

Heller, F. (2000) 'Creating a Holding Environment in an Inner City School.' In N. Barwick (ed.) *Clinical Counselling in Schools*. London: Routledge.

Hewitt, P. (2000) 'Confidentiality and Transference in School.' In N. Barwick (ed.) *Clinical Counselling in Schools*. London: Routledge.

Hinshelwood, R.D. (2001) *Thinking about Institutions: Milieux and Madness*. London: Jessica Kingsley Publishers.

Holmes, J. (2001) *The Search for the Secure Base: Attachment Theory and Psychotherapy*. Hove: Brunner-Routledge.

Hopper, E. (2003) *The Social Unconscious*. London: Jessica Kingsley Publishers.

Horne, A. (2006) 'Interesting Things to Say' in M. Lanyado and A. Horne (eds) *A Question of Technique*. Hove: Routledge.

Hurry, A. (1998) 'Psychoanalysis and Developmental Theory.' In A. Hurry (ed.) *Psychoanalysis and Developmental Theory*. London: Karnac Books.

Klein, M. (1946) 'Notes on Some Schizoid Mechanisms.' In M. Klein, P. Heimann, S. Isaacs and J. Riviere (eds) *Developments in Psychoanalysis*. London: Hogarth Press.

Knowles, E. (ed.) (2009) *Oxford Dictionary of Quotations* (7th edn). Oxford: Oxford University Press.

Knox, J. (2011) *Self-Agency in Psychotherapy: Attachment, Autonomy and Intimacy*. New York, NY, and London: W.W. Norton & Company.

Lanyado, M. (2004) *The Presence of the Therapist: Treating Childhood Trauma*. Hove and New York, NY: Routledge.

Lomas, P. (1987) *The Limits of Interpretation*. London: Constable.

Luxmoore, N. (2000) *Listening to Young People in School, Youth Work and Counselling*. London: Jessica Kingsley Publishers.

Luxmoore, N. (2002) 'Can We Do Something? Young People Using Action Methods to Support Each Other in School.' In A. Bannister and A. Huntington (eds) *Communicating with Children and Adolescents*. London: Jessica Kingsley Publishers.

Luxmoore, N. (2008) *Feeling Like Crap: Young People and the Meaning of Self-Esteem*. London: Jessica Kingsley Publishers.

Luxmoore, N. (2010) *Young People and the Curse of Ordinariness*. London: Jessica Kingsley Publishers.

Luxmoore, N. (2012) *Young People, Death and the Unfairness of Everything*. London: Jessica Kingsley Publishers.

Marzillier, J. (2010) *The Gossamer Thread: My Life as a Psychotherapist*. London: Karnac Books.

Mawson, C. (1994) 'Containing Anxiety in Work with Damaged Children.' In A. Obholzer and V. Zagier Roberts (eds) *The Unconscious at Work*. London: Routledge.

McGinnis, S. and Jenkins, P. (2011) *Good Practice Guidance for Counselling in Schools* (4th edn). Lutterworth: British Association for Counselling and Psychotherapy.

Menzies Lyth, I. (1988) *Containing Anxiety in Institutions*. London: Free Association Books.

Mowles, C. (2011) *Rethinking Management: Radical Insights from the Complexity Sciences*. Farnham: Gower Publishing.

Obholzer, A. and Zagier Roberts, V. (1994) 'Troublesome individual and troubled institution' in A. Obholzer and V. Zagier Roberts (eds) *The Unconscious at Work: Individual and Organisational Stress in the Human Services*. London: Routledge.

Ogden, T.H. (1986) *The Matrix of the Mind: Object Relations and the Psychoanalytic Dialogue*. Northvale, NJ, and London: Jason Aronson.

Ornstein, P.H. and Ornstein, A. (1994) 'On the conceptualisation of clinical facts in psychoanalysis.' *International Journal of Psycho-Analysis 75*, 977–94.

Phillips, A. (1994) *On Flirtation*. London: Faber.

Phillips, A. (2012) *Missing Out: In Praise of the Unlived Life*. London: Hamish Hamilton.

Pine, F. (1985) *Developmental Theory and Clinical Process*. New Haven, CT, and London: Yale University Press.

Pines, M. (1998) 'The Self as a Group, The Group as a Self.' In I.N.H. Harwood and M. Pines (eds) *Self Experiences in Group*. London: Jessica Kingsley Publishers.

Ruszczynski, S. (2007) 'The Problem of Certain Psychic Realities: Aggression and Violence as Perverse Solutions.' In D. Morgan and S. Ruszczynski (eds) *Lectures on Violence, Perversity and Delinquency*. London: Karnac Books.

Smith, K.K. and Berg, D.N. (1987) *Paradoxes of Group Life: Understanding Conflict, Paralysis, and Movement in Group Dynamics*. San Francisco, CA: Wiley.

Stokes, J. (1994) 'Institutional Chaos and Personal Stress.' In A. Obholzer and V. Zagier Roberts (eds) *The Unconscious at Work*. London: Routledge.

Winnicott, D.W. (1965) *The Maturational Processes and the Facilitating Environment*. London: Hogarth Press.

Winnicott, D.W. (1971) *Playing and Reality*. London: Routledge.

Winnicott, D.W. (1975) *Through Paediatrics to Psycho-Analysis*. London: Hogarth Press.

Yalom, I.D. (1980) *Existential Psychotherapy*. New York, NY: Basic Books.

INDEX

projection 15–16, 21, 51, 82, 98, 100,
    123–4
    see also projective identification
projective identification 13
    see also projection
psychoanalysis 16, 56
psychodynamic method 58
psychotherapy 36–7, 113, 139, 147

rage 71–2, 100
rape 80
recognition 103–4, 107–8, 126–7
referral(s) 30, 47
    forms 47–8, 50
revenge 31, 124, 128
rules 16, 46–7, 49, 62–3, 72, 92, 121,
    125, 128
Ruszczynski, S. 68, 76

sadness 40, 69, 125
secrecy 14, 16, 61
self
    belief 111
    confidence 102
    corridor 60
    counselling 60
    disclosure 62–3
    esteem 18, 108
    false 18, 81
    harm 13
    psychological 68
    true 18
separation 42, 53–4
sex, sexuality 13, 22, 43, 112, 139
    education 14
    life 111
shame 14, 21, 38, 42, 44, 59
Smith, K.K. 41
social workers 28
space between 59, 62
split, splitting 15, 18, 21, 74, 76–84, 91,
    114
Stokes, J. 82
stress 20, 68
suicide 41
superego 98
supervision 14, 70, 74–5, 102, 128–9,
    133, 149–50
Swift, Jonathan 22

time management 105
training 14, 16, 29, 35, 37, 135, 138, 147
    courses 11, 40, 42, 51, 53
    listening skills 19
    organization 54
    person-centred 58
transference 16, 54–6, 59, 62, 133
    counter 54–6, 59
    institutional 31
transparency 40

valency 13
volunteer counsellors 14, 56, 58, 130–1

waiting list 51, 57
Winnicott, D.W. 14, 59, 67, 93
work experience 102

Yalom, I.D. 72

Zagier Roberts, V. 30, 127